Alfred Hood

The Prophet of Nazareth, and His Message

Alfred Hood

The Prophet of Nazareth, and His Message

ISBN/EAN: 9783337036546

Printed in Europe, USA, Canada, Australia, Japan

Cover: Foto ©Lupo / pixelio.de

More available books at **www.hansebooks.com**

THE
PROPHET OF NAZARETH

AND

HIS MESSAGE.

BY THE REV.
ALFRED HOOD,
OF BOURNEMOUTH.

"*In things essential, unity; in things non-essential, liberty; in all things, charity.*"

LONDON:
SWAN SONNENSCHEIN, Le BAS & LOWREY,
PATERNOSTER SQUARE.
1886.

By the same Author.

THE LIFE AND TEACHING OF JESUS CHRIST,

TAKEN FROM THE SYNOPTIC GOSPELS.

TO FOLLOW SHORTLY.

SERMONS on the LORD'S PRAYER FOR YOUNG PEOPLE.

PREFACE.

The object of this little book is to unfold the essential elements of Christian Faith as set forth in the Message of Jesus, in the hope that solid ground for fellowship and union among all who profess and call themselves Christians may at length be found in the teaching of the great Prophet of Nazareth.

CONTENTS.

CHAP.		PAGE
I.	THE FORERUNNERS OF JESUS	1
II.	THE PROPHET'S METHOD OF TEACHING	12
III.	THE PRINCIPLES OF THE PROPHET OF NAZARETH	25
IV.	JESUS PROCLAIMS THE KINGDOM OF GOD	35
V.	THE COMMANDMENTS OF JESUS	45
VI.	THE FATHERHOOD OF GOD	55
VII.	THE BROTHERHOOD OF MAN	66
VIII.	THE LAST SUPPER	79
IX.	THE RELIGION OF HUMANITY	88
X.	THE FOLLOWERS OF JESUS	98

CHAPTER I.

THE FORERUNNERS OF JESUS.

No one can watch the growth and development of a little child without seeing that its physical nature unfolds itself first, then its intellect, and lastly its moral and spiritual powers. And what is true of each individual is also true concerning the race. In the lowest stages of civilisation brute force reigns supreme; and only as time rolls on do the intellect and the moral sense assert their rightful place among the nations. Hence we find that in the earliest ages religion appeals chiefly to the senses of man, then, later on, to his intellect, and lastly to his moral and spiritual insight; and for this reason we conclude that the older forms of religion, in which the sacrifice of animals plays so large a part, are lower than those forms which rest on intellectual dogmas, while these again are lower than those moral and spiritual forms of faith which are becoming ever more dominant in modern times. And, as some men have always advanced more rapidly than others, in all ages we witness a struggle between the older and the newer, the lower and the higher forms of religion; but nowhere, perhaps, can we study this conflict more readily than in the history of Judaism. All through the pages of the Old Testament indeed we find the priest, on the one hand, calling the people to the past, to the sensuous, to mere external forms and ceremonies; while, on the other hand, the prophet no less strenuously urges the people forward to that which is spiritual, to that which has its roots in the very heart of man. Inasmuch, however, as the older and lower form of faith preceded the newer and nobler, it possessed the authority of tradition, and the dead weight of custom. Nay, inasmuch as the older faith had its foundation laid in the dim, far-off past, the priests, either honestly or dishonestly, claimed a Divine sanction for their ordinances; and thus they became virtually the masters and rulers of the people, and even threatened them with the vengeance of God if they dared to disregard those forms and ceremonies which they proclaimed as necessary for the highest well-being of man. The best, therefore, of flocks and herds was set apart for what was called "Divine Service," the priests reserving to their own use the best of the best. But, at length, there arose a class of reformers who were not priests or ministers of the temple,* men who raised their voices on behalf of the people. For

* "The prophet comes forward among the Israelites as a servant and envoy of Jahveh, but he is no priest or temple minister. It is important to mark this, because out of Israel, in Egypt and in Greece, for instance, 'the prophet' belongs to the officers of the temple—a first proof that we must not allow ourselves to be misled by the name by which we are accustomed to

some time, it is true, the influence of these prophets of Israel is chiefly political. During the first century of the kingdom of Ephraim they are opposed to the government, and their sympathies are strongly democratic. Elijah is a demagogue; and Gad, the king's seer,* and Nathan, the tutor of young Solomon, withstand David to his face. But the later and truer prophets are more strictly religious in their influence. They are not afraid of kings, but they are not simply or chiefly political reformers. They are emphatically teachers of religion. They spare none who have done wrong; but their weapon is the sword of the Spirit, and their power is the power of integrity and uprightness. These are they who bring good tidings, who publish peace, who bring good tidings of good, who publish salvation, and say unto Zion, "Thy God reigneth." And they are "prophets," not because of any great capacity of foresight, but much rather by reason of their spiritual insight. The burden of their song is, Repent, reform, cease to do evil; learn to do well. What they desire is, not mere outward compliance with certain forms and ceremonies, nor the acceptance of this or that dogma, but righteousness of heart and life. Indeed, Jeremiah boldly proclaims the naked truth; and, in the name of

designate Israel's seers, and identify them with the men who are so called among other nations."—Kuenen's "Religion of Israel."

* The older prophets in Israel were called "seers;" but the true prophets, as F. W. Newman well remarks, were "men who professed to utter the voice of God, not to expound any sacred book, or rest upon any sacred law."

God, declares, "I spake not unto your fathers, nor commanded them, in the day that I brought them out of the land of Egypt, concerning burnt offerings or sacrifices; but this thing I commanded them, saying, Obey My voice, and I will be your God, and ye shall be My people." Here, then, we see that the prophet clearly maintains, in direct opposition to the whole doctrine of the priest, not only that God no longer requires either burnt offerings or sacrifices, not only that something else is more important than these forms, but that God did not institute them at all, even in the past; and, by implication, it follows that the prophet thought they were introduced by the priest. And we know that then, as now, the priests were a peculiar caste, a sort of close corporation, whose interests were more or less opposed to the interests of the people. We know that then, as now, and in all ages with but few exceptions, the priests, as a body, have been opposed to liberty and light, and to the genuine growth and true development of the community.*

But although Jeremiah alone goes to the root of the matter, and declares that there is no Divine sanction for the doctrine of sacrifices and offerings, yet other prophets, too, see the evil of the priestly teaching, and condemn it. Amos, for instance, says, "I hate, I despise your feasts, and have no delight in your

---

* "The priest is the developed sorcerer." See "Lectures on the Origin and Growth of Religion, as illustrated by the Native Religions of Mexico and Peru," by Albert Réville.

assemblies. Although ye offer Me burnt offerings and gifts, I will not accept them, and your thank-offerings of fatted calves I will not regard." Hosea, too, declares, "I desire mercy and not sacrifice, the knowledge of God more than burnt offerings." And Isaiah cries, "To what purpose is the multitude of your sacrifices unto Me? Wash you, make you clean. Put away the evil of your doings from before Mine eyes. Cease to do evil, learn to do well. Seek judgment; turn away the oppressor. Do justice to the fatherless; defend the cause of the widow." And in Micah we read, "Wherewith shall I come before Jehovah, and bow myself down before God on high? Shall I come before Him with burnt offerings, with the sacrifice of calves of a year old? Will Jehovah be pleased with thousands of rams, with ten thousands of rivers of oil? Shall I give my firstborn for my transgression, the fruit of my body for the sin of my soul? He hath showed thee, O man, what is good; and what doth Jehovah require of thee; what but to do justly, to love mercy, and to walk humbly with thy God?" And all the great forerunners of Jesus, down to His immediate predecessor, John the Baptist, wrought for the same great end,—the moral and spiritual regeneration of man. They were not priests, but prophets. They, therefore, called their hearers away from mere externals to the inner realities of life; and they sought to lead men everywhere to repent and mend their ways. They teach that no mere connection with any body corporate will avail for life, but only individual uprightness, only personal fidelity, the fruit of a holy spirit. "Bring forth, therefore, fruit worthy of repentance," says John,* "and think not to say within yourselves, We have Abraham to our father; for I say unto you, that God is able of these stones to raise up children unto Abraham. And even now is the axe laid unto the root of the trees; every tree, therefore, that bringeth not forth good fruit is hewn down, and cast into the fire."

And yet, in spite of these earnest appeals to the inner heart of man, many professed Christians still hark back to the priest instead of advancing with the prophet. As we should expect, there is most of this leaning on sacrificial forms in the communion of Rome, which prides itself on being the oldest Church in Christendom. But our own Establishment, in its Anglican revival, whilst also boasting of its antiquity, is lending its influence ever more and more in the same direction. In matters pertaining to religion, in this country at least, the power of the priest seems to be on the increase. Even so-called "orthodox" Dissent, though protesting equally against the assumptions of Rome and of our own Episcopal Church, still lends itself to the evil influence of priestcraft; for the very essence of so-called "orthodoxy" lies in the belief that God *did* ordain sacrifices and offerings, culminating at

---

* John the Baptist was one of the exceptions that prove the rule; but, though he was of a priestly family, he wrought not in the temple service, but as a prophet.

last in the Cross of Calvary. This "orthodoxy," therefore, in all its forms, though in various degrees, sides with the priests and not with the prophets, and thus is directly opposed to Jesus, the last and chiefest Prophet of Israel. "Christianity," says the author of "Natural Religion," "in its original character had an evident analogy with that modern liberal movement which assails Catholicism. It breathed something of the spirit of equality, and still more of the spirit of fraternity; it took its rise in a bold rebellion against sacerdotal authority." But why was the newer faith thus opposed, *in its earliest form*, to all sacerdotal authority? It was because Jesus was emphatically no priest, but a Prophet. Everywhere and always was He opposed to priestcraft. Never, indeed, does Jesus mention a priest to praise him, but most certainly to condemn. The priests of His day could see clearly that His teaching and influence (before they were perverted by later ages) were calculated to destroy their power root and branch. Hence they were ever opposed to Him in deadly conflict. We read, therefore, that the priests "sought how they might have Him with subtilty and kill Him." It was they, too, who "sought false witness against Jesus." It was the priests who "bound Him and led Him away, and delivered Him up to Pilate, the governor;" and when Jesus stood before the governor it was the chief priest who accused Him. And, finally, it was the priests who "persuaded the multitudes that they should ask for Barabbas, and destroy Jesus." Are not all these things written in our Gospels? But, sacerdotal as was the Jewish form of religion, it allowed more liberty to the people in their worship than does the Church of Rome or our own Episcopal Establishment; for every time that Jesus stood up in the synagogue to read, and address words of exhortation to His fellow-worshippers, He spoke *not* as a priest, nor even as a scribe, but as a layman.

I have said that Jesus never mentions a priest to praise him, but most certainly to condemn. And yet, over and over again, He extols both the prophet and the prophet's office. "He that receiveth a prophet in the name of a prophet" (*i.e.*, because he is a prophet) "shall receive a prophet's reward," said Jesus. And again, "A prophet is not without honour, save in his own country and in his own house." Everywhere, too, throughout the Gospels, is Jesus called a "prophet," but never a priest. When Herod "would have put Him to death, he feared the multitude, because they counted Him a prophet." We read also, "A great prophet is arisen among us." And, speaking of Himself, Jesus says, "It cannot be that a prophet perish out of Jerusalem." But why does Jesus thus single out Jerusalem for this equivocal honour? Does not the Psalmist speak of the city of God as "beautiful for situation, the joy of the whole earth"? Do we not read that "in Salem also is His tabernacle, and His dwelling-place in Zion"? Yea, verily, but Jerusalem was also by pre-eminence the place of the priests. And this is the reason why Jesus was compelled to say, "It cannot be that a prophet perish out of Jerusalem." It was the priests who at every turn were His opponents while He trod this earth; and in every succeeding age it has still been the priests who have covered over His teaching by their traditions. And now, in this latest age, in the light of past history and present experience, the question is pressed upon us with ever-increasing force, Can a man be both a priest and a Christian? Do we not see that the priest and the prophet in every age stand opposed to one another? Can there be any doubt, therefore, that the more of the priest there is in any man, the less there is of the Christian? The prophets, through all time, have helped men to approach God; but in every period of history the priests, as middle men, have stood between the Great Good Spirit and His children. The prophets have ever exalted the character of God, and have sought to lead men to become somewhat like the All-Wise, the All-True, the All-Good, that Parent and children may be as one; but the priests have as persistently fostered the degrading thought that God, through their influence, may be bribed, bought by a present, and thus turned aside from His righteous ways to commit injustice.*

---

* The priest, as Walter Besant says, requires "knowledge of human nature and ability to use that knowledge." But the prophet must not only know what is in man, but he must *love* man. The priest may use man to forward his own schemes, but the prophet is willing to spend and be spent for the good of man.

And the religion of this age contains a mixture of the truths proclaimed by the prophets and the errors promulgated by the priests. We are still in a transitional stage, and have not yet dared to stand, like Jesus, in opposition to those false sayings which have ever been said to them of old times. Many who profess and call themselves Christians still appeal to the priestly teaching of the past, and build their beliefs on ancient traditions; and even those who rise above the sensuous elements of priestcraft often dwell on the necessity of mere dogmas of the intellect, as though they were of vital importance to religion. But God has left no age without the witness of His Spirit; and, in every nation, he that feareth God and worketh righteousness is accepted of Him. Nevertheless, even until this day, priest and prophet still exist side by side, though, as of old, frequently in conflict; and many, in opposition to the prophets, and, therefore, in opposition to Jesus, continue to trust in mere forms and ceremonies, and in what they deem correct opinion as necessary for salvation both here and in the life to come. And, for the present, it would almost seem that the priests have once more won the day. But surely the time of the prophet is at hand, and Jesus will yet vanquish error, and lead men up to God. For it is the prophets of Israel, and chiefly her greatest son —Jesus of Nazareth—who have helped us to-day to feel that there is a Holy Power or Influence within us, though not of us—"a power not ourselves, which makes for righteousness." And we feel it is this Spirit which, in spite of our waywardness, our littleness, our ignorance, yea, in spite of our selfishness and sin, helps us onward and upward day by day, and is the cause of all our growth in holiness, in truth, in love. It is the prophets who tell us what real religion is, and not the priests; and they tell us that it consists, not in sacrifices and offerings, not in forms and ceremonies, but in justice, mercy, and fidelity. It is the prophets, those sons of God, who speak to us across the centuries, who best teach us to do justly, to love mercy, and to walk humbly with our God. It was His son Jesus, the greatest of all the prophets, Who declared us also to be sons of God, and showed us how we could live as His children.

> "Thou Who in life below
> Didst drain the cup of woe,
> And glorify the cross of agony,—
> Thy blessed labours done,
> Thy crown of victory won,
> Hast passed from earth—passed to Thy home on high.
>
> "It was no path of flowers,
> Through this dark world of ours,
> Beloved of the Father, Thou didst tread;
> And shall we in dismay
> Shrink from the narrow way,
> When clouds and darkness are around it spread?

CHAPTER II.

THE PROPHET'S METHOD OF TEACHING.

MATTHEW ARNOLD, in "Literature and Dogma," says:—If we describe the work of Christ by a short expression which may give the clearest view of it, we shall describe it thus, that He came to restore the intuition of God through transforming the idea of righteousness; and that to do this He brought a method, and He brought a secret. But I have no intention, at present, of dwelling upon what Matthew Arnold regards as Christ's "method" of arriving at peace. I simply desire in this chapter to point out what I consider to be the method which Jesus adopted in unfolding His teaching to the people. I want to show by what method He rose above the narrow thought and feeling of His day and generation, so that we also by the same method may rise above the superstitions of modern times. And the first thing which we may notice in His teaching is, that it was selective. We constantly find Jesus dwelling upon what was noblest and best in the teaching of His forerunners, and rejecting what He deemed unworthy and untrue. On that memorable Sabbath day, when He stood up to read in the synagogue of His own native village of Nazareth, there was delivered to Him the book of the prophet Isaiah, though, from the account in the third Gospel, it appears that Jesus did not approve of all He met with even in the writings of this great prophet. For, after the words, "To proclaim the acceptable year of the Lord," with which Jesus closes His reading, we find in Isaiah the following words also, "And the day of vengeance of our God." But Jesus, it would seem, had no desire to speak on such a theme as this; and so He stops short without making any mention of "vengeance" at all. Hence His method of teaching was selective; for He insisted on what He felt was good, and quietly let fall what He did not approve. The bee appears to sip honey from every flower; but, though it visits very many blossoms, it only gathers its food here and there. Thus also the prophet, though familiar with the teaching of all the ages, insists alone on what is good and true.

The method which Jesus adopted in His teaching, however, was not simply selective; not only did He choose what He felt was good, and reject what He thought was bad from the olden doctrines, but He was by no means "bound" to the past alone. Sometimes He would extend, and sometimes intensify the teaching delivered to the fathers. "Ye have heard that it was said to them of old time, Thou shalt not kill; and whosoever shall kill shall be in danger of the judgment; but I say unto you, that every one who is angry with his brother (without a cause) shall be in danger of the judgment." And, again, we read, "Ye have heard that it was said, Thou shalt not commit adultery; but I say unto you, that every one that looketh on a woman to lust after her hath committed adultery with her already in his heart." And sometimes, too, we find that Jesus reverses the popular teaching of His day; for we further read, " Ye have heard that it was said, Thou shalt love thy neighbour, and hate thine enemy; but I say unto you, Love your enemies, and pray for them that persecute you, that ye may be sons of your Father Who is in heaven."

Nor should we pass by unnoticed another feature in the method which this great Prophet adopted in His teaching, for constantly do we see that He emphasises the spirit rather than the letter of the ancient scriptures of His people. There is an example of this in the passage of the Gospel to which I have just referred, wherein Jesus points out that sin lies in an evil thought or desire of the heart, as well as in a more formal breaking of the Jewish law. We read, too, in so many words, "Woe unto you, scribes and Pharisees, hypocrites, for ye tithe mint and anise and cummin, and have left undone the weightier matters of the law, judgment and mercy and faith." Indeed, the Prophet of Nazareth, it would appear, differed from the teachers of His day chiefly in this,—they cared especially for outward conformity to the ceremonial law, while for this He cared little or nothing; He, on the other hand, valued the inner life and spirit of the law, while they took no notice of it. Hence, while a modern scholar* is able to say it is certain that it was His "bold defiance of the law of Moses, partly as it was in itself, partly as interpreted by scribes and Pharisees, that brought Jesus to the cross," yet in the first Gospel we read, "Think not that I came to destroy the law or the prophets; I came not to destroy, but to fulfil." From His own explicit teaching concerning the Sabbath, and likewise from His own personal conduct, we see clearly how little regard Jesus paid to any *formal* observance of the law, when by disregarding the form he could be true to a higher duty still ; and, as we shall subsequently see, He maintained that both the law and prophets are fulfilled by love. "All things, therefore, whatsoever ye would that men should do to you, even so do ye also unto them, for this is the law and the prophets." It is, then, inner reality, not outward form, that Jesus ever desired. "Woe unto you, scribes and Pharisees, hypocrites, for ye cleanse the outside of the cup and of the platter, but within they are full from extortion and excess. Thou blind Pharisee, cleanse first the inside of the cup and of the platter, that the outside thereof may become clean also. Woe unto you, scribes and Pharisees, hypocrites, for ye are like unto whited sepulchres, which outwardly appear beautiful, but inwardly are full of dead men's bones and all uncleanness. Even so ye also outwardly appear righteous

* "The Gospel according to Paul." By the Rev. E. M. Geldart, M.A.

unto men, but inwardly ye are full of hypocrisy and iniquity." In the same spirit, too, Jesus says to His disciples, "Except your righteousness shall exceed the righteousness of the scribes and Pharisees, ye shall in no wise enter into the kingdom of heaven." So little, indeed, did Jesus approve of outward show that He says, "Take heed that ye do not your righteousness before men, to be seen of them, else ye have no reward with your Father Who is in heaven." And again, "When thou doest alms let not thy left hand know what thy right hand doeth; that thy alms may be in secret, and thy Father, Who seeth in secret, shall recompense thee. And when ye pray, ye shall not be as the hypocrites, for they love to stand and pray in the synagogues and in the corners of the streets, that they may be seen of men. Verily, I say unto you, they have received their reward. But thou, when thou prayest, enter into thine inner chamber, and, having shut thy door, pray to thy Father, Who is in secret, and thy Father, Who seeth in secret, shall recompense thee." Thus we find that the method of teaching which Jesus adopted, whether He addressed the people at large or His immediate disciples, was not the method of the priest, but the method of the prophet. He gives no minute instructions concerning sacraments and ordinances or laying on of hands. He gives no commandments concerning special celebrations or sacred festivals. He valued not the forms and ceremonies of religion, nor its dogmas, but life and conduct, which, growing out of a Divine love, should unite man to man and earth to heaven. His appeal, therefore, was not made to the tradition of the past, but to the living hearts and consciences of His hearers. Nor was it simply to His disciples, but to the multitude that He said, "When ye see a cloud rising in the west, straightway ye say there cometh a shower, and so it cometh to pass. And when ye see a south wind, ye say there will be a scorching heat, and it cometh to pass. Ye hypocrites, ye know how to interpret the face of the earth and the heaven, but how is it that ye know not how to interpret these times? And why even of yourselves judge ye not what is right?"

"When Jesus came," says James Freeman Clarke, "He found that the Jewish priest had silenced the Jewish prophet. No prophet had appeared in Judea for four hundred years, but the sacraments, sacrifices, and temple worship went on as before. These services had stiffened into lifeless form; so the first time that Jesus entered the temple, He drove out the money-changers, and said, 'You have made My Father's house a den of thieves.' They had made an idol of the Temple; He said that every stone should be pulled down. They had made an idol of the Sabbath; He said, 'The Sabbath is made for man.' They had made an idol of sacrificial offerings; He said, 'God will have mercy, and not sacrifice.' They had made an idol of solemn public prayers; He said, 'When thou prayest, go into thy closet.' He denounced the scribes and Pharisees, who, for pretence, made long prayers, and by their cold formal hypocrisy shut up the kingdom of heaven against men. He said that the pure in heart saw God face to face, and that the true worshippers did not worship the Father in this place or that, but in spirit and truth." Thus, what the Prophet of Nazareth sought was not simply to purify the older faith of His people. This He desired to do in common with all other great religious reformers; but His chief desire seems to have been to elevate religion by raising the character of man. Other teachers had said to men, You cannot approach God for yourself, for you are not yet good enough, and must, therefore, get the priest to pray for you. And to-day, even the ultra-Protestant, who by no means desires to exalt the office of the priest, affirms that the children of God cannot approach the great Father of us all in their own right, and that, therefore, Christ must act as mediator between God and man. But the Prophet from Galilee said nothing of this sort. He knew, as we know, that man is anything but too good; but He never argued, as many have done since, that, therefore, somebody more holy than the ordinary run of people must do something for man, in order that he may be able to approach God. On the contrary, Jesus worked not from without, but from within. He seemed to say, Though what men *do* is important, very important, yet what they *are* is even more important still, if that be possible. He, therefore, did not seek to reform man by reforming religion so much as to reform religion by reforming man. His first intention is ever to make man good; and He evidently thought and taught that man could best be made good, not by forcing him away from the source of all goodness through the instrumentality of a mediator, but by bringing him nearer and still nearer to God. Thus we find that this great Prophet at once reversed the tendency of all earlier forms of faith, and quickened religion into newer life. Never did He teach that man must reach perfection before he can approach God. He set no impossible task to His disciples. He asked for no deeds beyond the achievement of man. But He taught that, if man really desires in the sincerity of his heart to do right and to be good, though his action might halt behind his wish, he should see Him Who is invisible. "Blessed are the pure in heart; for they shall see God." Always and ever did Jesus insist on this doctrine of inwardness, knowing that where the heart is right, all else in time will follow.

And appealing thus straight to the thoughts and feelings of His hearers, like a true prophet, Jesus pointed out to them, and to us, the road to growth and progress. The priest, in all ages, in as far as he is a priest, regards inspiration and revelation as things of the past; and, therefore, has no word of life for the present. He points to what is established; and, simply because it is established, regards it as sacred, and of Divine appointment. But the prophet looks not only to the past and to the present, but also to the future, and reveres alone that which is in itself good and true. By a Divine insight he sees that which, apart from age or clime, is pure, noble, and right. True, we read in the Sermon on the Mount, "Verily I say unto you, Till heaven and earth pass away, one jot or one tittle shall in no wise pass away from the law, till all things be accomplished." But we have already seen, in the case of the Sabbath, that it was not the external form of any mere ceremonial law which Jesus deemed binding on the conscience; and in so many words we read, "The Sabbath was made for man, and not man for the Sabbath." We have, moreover, referred to a passage in the same Sermon on the Mount, wherein Jesus even reverses the teaching of some of those who had preceded Him; "Ye have heard that it was said, Thou shalt love thy neighbour, and hate thine enemy; but I say unto you, Love your enemies." And thus do we see clearly that in the teaching of the Prophet of Nazareth His method was a method of progress. Not that Jesus broke with the past, for He stood in the true line of the great prophets of Israel. In the fourth chapter of our third Gospel we find that He illustrates His teaching from the works of the prophets; and, indeed, that He identifies Himself with their class, by speaking of Himself as one of them: "No prophet is acceptable in his own country." The work of His disciples, too, He regards not as the work of priests, but as the work of prophets; for at the end of the Beatitudes we read, "Blessed are ye when men shall reproach you, and persecute you, and say all manner of evil against you falsely, for My sake. Rejoice, and be exceeding glad; for great is your reward in heaven; for so persecuted they the prophets which were before you." And, in looking back over the past history of His people, Jesus felt that He also, like His forerunners, had met with the fate of the prophets. "O Jerusalem, Jerusalem, thou that killest the prophets, and stonest them that are sent unto thee, how often would I have gathered thy children together, even as a hen gathereth her chickens under her wings, and ye would not." And why was it even so? Because men have too often preferred to receive their religious instruction "cut and dried," and put into some compact form; so that they may, without trouble, be able to talk about it in set phrase, and so appear to know more than they really do. Therefore, in the nineteenth century as in the first, too many men "say, and do not." But, in the teaching of Jesus, there is no appeal to any authority outside man as final and binding on the human conscience, whether it be Church, Book, or Priest; for this is not the method of the prophet. In all that Jesus taught we see a steady and a firm reliance on human nature, aided alone by the great Spirit of Truth and Holiness and Love; for He knew that the faithful heart of God's own children would bear witness to the truth which He proclaimed. Ever do we find in the teaching of Jesus that His method is the method of the prophet—a method which leads men into living faith and personal holiness, and thus into the presence of the Fountain of all wisdom, goodness, and truth, where alone they can hold communion with the Father of spirits, the God of Love. And surely herein the Prophet of Nazareth was before His time; for, as Francis William Newman says,* "antiquity certainly had not learned that private men had any *right to a conscience* of their own in religion. The main reason was this. Religion, in their idea, was essentially external and corporate, not individual, personal, internal, as Jesus in every utterance assumes it to be. He never dilates on the covenant of Jehovah with *collective* Israel, but dwells on the relation of each separate worshipper to a Father in heaven as a private affair. This was the fruitful germ, this was the 'seed of mustard' by which He virtually called His countrymen to free thinking concerning their national institutions." Indeed, as that excellent book, "The Bible for Young People," so beautifully says: "By His own experience He had come to know that God is our Father, that He is Love; for He had experienced the indescribably sweet and irresistible attraction, the unutterably blessed influence of that sacred Power above us Which unfolds Its Will in the human heart and conscience; He had 'tasted and seen' that unreserved obedience to this Will is

* "Christianity in its Cradle."

the fullest life, the purest joy; that communion with this God is peace to our souls." Yes, this is the method of the true prophet; for he speaks alone that which he knows—that which he knows by personal experience. His doctrine is not his, but the Father's. It is not reached through logic, or any of the metaphysical refinements of the schools; it is not the result of philosophy; but comes down from the Father of lights upon the true and faithful spirit; for the pure in heart see God.

We have seen, then, in looking over the teaching of Jesus, that His method was selective; for He marked out for approval what He deemed good among the sayings of the olden times, and rejected as unworthy what He felt was evil. We have found, too, that He was in no way "bound" by the past, that He not simply chose what He thought well from the ancient scriptures, but that in some cases He extended and intensified the teaching of former generations, while in other cases He even reversed that teaching. We have also observed that He emphasised, not the letter, but the spirit of the earlier teaching, and placed uprightness of heart before outward ceremonial observance. "But, if ye had known what this meaneth,—I desire mercy and not sacrifice, ye would not have condemned the guiltless. For the Son of Man * is Lord of the Sabbath." Although Jesus did not break with the past, but stood in the great line

* "Son of Man" is a prophet's title, occurring in Ezekiel alone over ninety times.

of the prophets, we found that His method was the method of growth and progress, of nature and of life. And in all past ages, throughout the whole region of created being, every step in the upward path of life seems to have been achieved by means of this method, and apart from it there would appear to be no real growth and progress open to man. We might perchance lead what some would deem very good lives by following the teaching of the priests, and walking in the footsteps of preceding generations; but, if we believe that man is still capable of further growth and progress, if we desire this growth and progress for our own souls, we must learn the method of the prophet, and choose for ourselves,—choose, as did Jesus, wisely and well. And if we would help the ages yet to come, we must apply His method to the religion of our day and generation, as boldly and as fearlessly as He applied it to the religion of His times; for our spiritual life depends upon our following this method of the great Prophet Son of God.

> "O Thou great Friend to all the sons of men,
>   Who once appeared in humblest guise below,
> Sin to rebuke, to break the captive's chain,
>   And call Thy brethren forth from want and woe!
>
> We look to Thee; Thy truth is still the light
>   Which guides the nations, groping on their way,
> Stumbling and falling in disastrous night,
>   Yet hoping ever for the perfect day.
>
> Yes! Thou art still the Life; Thou art the Way
>   The holiest know;—Light, Life, and Way of heaven!
> And they who dearest hope, and deepest pray,
>   Toil by the light, life, way, which Thou hast given."
>
>   THEODORE PARKER.

CHAPTER III.

THE PRINCIPLES OF THE PROPHET OF NAZARETH.

In speaking of the method which was pursued by the Prophet of Nazareth, we found that He neither broke away from the past, nor was fettered by it, but always felt Himself free to select what He thought was most worthy in earlier teaching, and at times even to reverse or pass beyond the thoughts of prior ages. And He was willing that other men should do the same; for He appealed to the living voice of conscience, and desired that His hearers should receive, or reject, His message, according as it was vouched for by the human heart. "Why judge ye not of yourselves what is right?" Hence, while often disregarding outward forms, He always and everywhere insisted on the inner truth which they enshrined. Never did He emphasise the letter, but always the spirit. He desired not dogma, but life,—a life of holiness, which ever leads to peace. But, before we proceed to note what are the special doctrines which He inculcated, let us consider what are the principles which underlie His teaching. These principles, I take it, are three: first, Repentance; then,

Faith; and, as the crown of all, Love. We shall see, subsequently, that the outer form of the teaching of Jesus took shape in the proclamation of the Kingdom of God among men; but this proclamation was associated both with faith and with repentance. In the third chapter of our first Gospel we read that John the Baptist, as a forerunner of the Prophet of Nazareth, also preached about "the coming kingdom." And certain it is that both prophets are represented as commencing their message by calling their hearers to repentance; but Jesus went further than John, and dwelt on the need also of faith, and still more on the necessity for love.* But what did Jesus mean by repentance? "Of the Greek word 'metanoia,'" says Matthew Arnold— "we translate it repentance, a mourning and lamenting over one's sins; and we translate it wrong—of 'metanoia,' as Jesus used the word, the lamenting one's sins was a small part; the main part was something far more active and fruitful, the setting up an immense new inward movement for obtaining the rule of life. And 'metanoia' accordingly is a change of the inner man." Here, then, is the first principle in all vital religion. And hence we find that the Galilean Prophet always appealed to that which is within. "Cleanse first the inside of the cup and of the platter, that the outside thereof may become clean also." "The things which

---

* "With John, however, the duty of repentance, with Jesus the promise of forgiveness, had the greater prominence."—*See* "The Gospel according to Paul," by the Rev. E. M. Geldart.

proceed out of the mouth come forth out of the heart; and they defile the man." Therefore, there must be "a change of the inner man." And, if there was one evil more than another that was condemned by this Prophet of Nazareth, it was insincerity. That a man should be one thing outwardly, and another thing inwardly, was ever abhorrent to the mind of Jesus. "Beware ye of the leaven of the Pharisees, which is hypocrisy." "Woe unto you, scribes and Pharisees, hypocrites, for ye are like whited sepulchres, which outwardly appear beautiful, but inwardly are full of dead men's bones, and of all uncleanness. Even so ye appear righteous unto men, but inwardly ye are full of hypocrisy and iniquity." Hence Jesus desired, as a preliminary to all else, "a change of the inner man." What He required was righteousness within; and this involves repentance, for we must leave the wrong before we can truly serve the right. With this great Teacher everything depends on fidelity of heart and conscience, since rectitude springs out of the inner man. "Judge not according to appearance; but judge righteous judgment." "Except your righteousness shall exceed the righteousness of the scribes and Pharisees" (which was an external righteousness), "ye shall in no wise enter into the kingdom of God." No mere attendance at public worship, nor knowledge of the Scriptures, nor profession of belief, nor observance of religious customs, avails with Jesus apart from "a change of the inner man." And yet just as many in His day trusted to their being children of Abraham, so now many trust to their baptism, but now, as then, neglect judgment, mercy, and fidelity. Nay, even those who lament their shortcomings, and mourn over their sins, sometimes stop short of real repentance, of any radical change within. But it is not enough to know that one has done wrong; it is not enough to be sorry for past transgressions; there must be an *active* change from within; there must be a fresh growth in the heart; there must be a setting up of a " new inward movement for obtaining the rule of life," before there is any true repentance according to the teaching of Jesus. As a plant, which is cut down, because it has not done well, starts afresh into more vigorous life, so man must actively and resolutely turn from wrong, and grow afresh in his inward parts, if he would follow Jesus and truly live. For the repentance which He insisted on is the first step to eternal life,—a life of faith and love.

But just as the word " repentance " has been limited in its meaning, as though it referred only to sorrow for sin, so the word " faith " has also been degraded, and made to signify the mere acceptance of a set form of belief. It is true that the Galilean Prophet, in proclaiming the kingdom, says, " Believe in the good news." But the good news here spoken of consists simply in one fact,—the fact that there is, and that, too, close at hand, a kingdom of God, a kingdom of righteousness and peace; and what Jesus, in this proclamation, desires is personal loyalty to Him, Who rules in righteousness and love. And, moreover, in this case as in the case of repentance, if we look at the Greek words translated "believe" and "faith," we shall find that they too have a fuller meaning than is commonly supposed; for these words signify "trust," primarily trust in a person; and their secondary meaning is "fidelity," "faithfulness." What a far-reaching principle of religion, then, have we here! We may say in our day, as Jesus said in His, God, the Wise, the True, the Good, the All-Wise, the All-True, the All-Good, verily rules among the children of men. The times may seem dark (though they cannot well seem darker than they were in Judea during the first century); men may appear unjust (though they are not more unjust now than in times past);—but, come what may, there is one fact that underlies all other facts: this world belongs to God, and He rules supreme. One cannot therefore sow evil, and reap good; nor can one sow good, and reap evil. Man may deceive, but God never. Here is a sufficient reason for trusting God with firm and true allegiance:

> "For right is right, since God is God;
> And right the day must win;
> To doubt would be disloyalty,
> To falter would be sin."

Eighteen centuries and a half have rolled on since the great Prophet of Nazareth proclaimed this "Gospel;" and it is as true now as ever. Nay, it has almost ceased to be a mere matter of faith; for it ever becomes more and more a fact,—a fact which comes within the range of most certain knowledge. The more man learns about either the physical or the spiritual world, the more clearly does he see that there is nothing uncertain under the sun; "but all things hold their march, as if by one great will." Nay more; for, as George Eliot has so truly said, "We reap what we sow; but nature has love over and above that justice, and gives us shadow, and blossom, and fruit, that spring from no planting of ours."

Notwithstanding, however, this certainty that God rules, and that, therefore, the good and the true never deceive; notwithstanding the fact that none have ever done right without receiving the due reward of uprightness, since God has joined together peace and righteousness,—so joined them that no one can put them asunder; yet, even in these latest days, many are often still distrustful, and have but little faith. But why is it so but because they lack in love, and so are not like God? For, although I have placed "love" as the third, as the last great principle in the teaching of the Prophet of Nazareth, it is, in truth, the chief among them all. It is the deepest, and the most far-reaching principle in every form of religion, and it underlies all that is holiest and best on earth as in heaven. Even as faith reaches upward to God, and includes trust in Him, as well as fidelity to His children, so love includes reverence for the All-Perfect, as well as service to the imperfect. Yes, love not only embraces reverence, which is the foundation of all religion God-ward; but it also, on its earthward side, involves sacrifice for the good of others.

> "For we must share, if we would keep
> That blessing from above :
> Ceasing to give, we cease to have;
> Such is the law of love."

Hence, in a sense, it may be equally true to say that love, or that sacrifice, is the heart and soul of the teaching of Jesus; to proclaim that love, or that sacrifice, is the vital principle that ran through His life's work; to affirm that love, or that sacrifice, is the true mark of His disciples in all ages, and, therefore, now. But, inasmuch as we are told explicitly, "By this shall all men know that ye are My disciples, if ye have love one towards another," it is better, perhaps, to speak of love as the broader principle, including self-sacrifice, rather than to speak of self-sacrifice as including love, the more so, too, because Jesus not only sums up the law and prophets, *i.e.*, the whole of religion, in love, and thus includes the Ten Words in His two great commandments, but also tells the lawyer, who stood up and tempted Him, that through love man must live. Is it not true, then, that love is the most vital principle in religion, if there is no life without love?

> "They sin who tell us love can die;
> With life all other passions fly,
> All others are but vanity;
> In heaven ambition cannot dwell,
> Nor avarice in the haunts of hell;
> Earthly these passions of the earth,
> They perish where they have their birth :
> But love is indestructible."

Here, then, is the innermost shrine in true Christianity; for love is the life-stream which flowed through the all-glorious deeds and words of the great Nazarene. The disciples, it is true, often misunderstood the teaching of their Master; and once, indeed, He had to rebuke two of them for departing from this principle of love. But so emphatic did the teaching of the Prophet of Nazareth become on this vital point as it unfolded itself, that the writings of His earliest followers are more or less pervaded by this same sentiment. For, although they sometimes depart from His teaching, yet on this question of love they are as true as steel. Here Jesus was so explicit that none could possibly mistake Him, so emphatic that none could pervert His message. Hence the grandest utterances in the New Testament, outside the actual words of Jesus, are written concerning love. "Beloved," says the First Epistle of John, "let us love one another; for love is of God; and every one that loveth is born of God, and knoweth God. He that loveth not knoweth not God, for God is love." And, in the First Epistle to the Corinthians, we read, "Though I speak with the tongues of men and angels, and have not love, I am become as sounding brass, or a tinkling cymbal. And though I have the gift of prophecy, and understand all mysteries, and all knowledge; and though I have all faith, so that I could remove mountains, and have not love, I am nothing. And though I bestow all my goods to feed the poor, and though I give my body to be burned, and have not love, it profiteth me nothing. Love suffereth long and is kind; love envieth not; love vaunteth not itself, is not puffed up, doth not behave itself unseemly, seeketh not her own, is not easily provoked, thinketh no evil; rejoiceth not in iniquity, but rejoiceth in the truth; beareth all things, believeth all things, hopeth all things, endureth all things. Love never faileth."

Thus we see that three great principles underlie the teaching of the great Prophet of Nazareth,—Repentance, which involves more than sorrow for sin, and includes "a change of the inner man;" Faith, which embraces trust in God and fidelity to man; Love, love of God and love of man, which cannot exist apart from a willingness to sacrifice oneself for the good of others. And these three great principles are the foundation of all true religion. Nor can they be separated without destroying the whole superstructure. Unless man is to be the sole exception throughout the entire realm of nature; unless man is willing to stand still, while all things else progress,—he must, time after time, and again and again, repent: the inner mind of man, yea of the noblest and the best as well as of the least worthy, must change, and change until it reaches perfection. For it is not possible that any should be able really and fully to trust God, or be utterly faithful to man, apart from this inner change, unless there be a daily turning away from evil towards the good. And, without this "change of the inner man," without trust in God, without fidelity to man, none can truly love.

"Try us, O God, and search the ground
    Of every sinful heart;
Whate'er of sin in us is found,
    O bid it all depart."

"O God! the pure alone,
    E'en in their deep confessing,
Can see Thee as their own,
    And find the perfect blessing:
Yet to each waiting soul
    Speak in Thy still small voice,
Till broken love's made whole,
    And saddened hearts rejoice."

CHAPTER IV.

JESUS PROCLAIMS THE KINGDOM OF GOD.

JESUS of Nazareth was born and bred a Jew; He was brought up in the religion of His fathers. Indeed, so far as we can gather from His life, He never separated Himself from the communion of Israel or sought to establish any new form of faith. His doctrines, therefore, were the doctrines of Judaism. It is true, as we have already seen, that the method of His teaching was selective, that He constantly emphasised what was noblest and best in the teaching of His forerunners, and rejected or passed by what He deemed unworthy. It is true, as we have also seen, not only that His method was selective, but that He was in no way "bound" by the past; that He sometimes extended and intensified earlier teachings, dwelling always on the spirit rather than on the letter of the ancient scriptures of His people. Thus it comes to pass that the spiritual elements of religion are ever supreme throughout the teaching of this great Prophet. If, for example, we examine the Sermon on the Mount, we find an entire absence of what are called "dogmas" or "articles" of religion; but, on the contrary, we see everywhere deep spiritual truths, which appeal directly to the heart and conscience of all good men and true. The disciples of Jesus, we find, are to "hunger and thirst after righteousness;" they are to be "merciful," to be "peacemakers," to be "pure in heart." And so everywhere does this Prophet of Nazareth insist on that which is spiritual; ever does He make religion depend on righteousness of heart and life, not on assent to mere opinion.

But although Jesus laid so little stress on what we now call "dogma," and although He never appears to have introduced any new "beliefs" into religion, yet we find that He did none the less lay special stress on certain doctrines, upon which, it seems, He desired to build the faith of His disciples. According to the Second Gospel, as soon as John the Baptist was removed from the scene of his labours, Jesus came forward and preached to the men of Galilee. And this first message, as we should expect, dwelt not on the doctrine of the priests, but on the special doctrine of the prophets. The Prophet of Nazareth proclaimed the kingdom of God. But this was not only the first doctrine which He taught; it was the doctrine which was ever present to His mind. This was the foundation upon which all else that He taught was built. Paul, the great missionary to the Gentiles, preached Christ; but Jesus, the Prophet from Galilee, from first to last preached not Himself, but God and His kingdom. I have said that the doctrines of Jesus were the doctrines of Judaism, and, therefore, we find that this idea of a kingdom was not at all new to the Jews, but had all through the ages been dwelt upon, more or less, by their prophets. Before the time of Samuel there was no recognised earthly king among the children of Israel; but God was looked upon as their King in heaven. The creation of a king in Israel, we read, was regarded by the prophets as opposed to the will of Jehovah. Accordingly it was thought that, on the return from the captivity, the Lord would go before the people like an Eastern monarch, for whom every valley was to be exalted and every mountain and hill made low, that the glory of the Lord might be revealed. So, too, we learn from the Book of Daniel that, during the time of the Maccabees, in the second century B.C., there was again no earthly king in Israel, but a firm belief in the presence of the heavenly King. And when Pompey appeared on the scene at a still later time, to act as arbitrator in the civil wars of the Jews, a deputation of the people told him they did not wish to be governed by kings. But neither did the people desire to be ruled by foreigners, for they had too frequently suffered from the yoke of strangers, which was ever the source of many of their greatest troubles.

Now, in the time of Jesus this evil of foreign government was lying only too heavily upon His fellow-countrymen. Their political liberty was extinguished. The poor were oppressed by the publicans, who collected the Roman taxes, and were often unjust in their exactions. And although the people were free to worship God after the manner of their forefathers, yet they appear to have been demoralised by the unhappy times in which their lot was cast, and many of them were living according to their own will, while disregarding the rule of God. Religion had become so ritualistic, so much a matter of forms to be gone through, that the ceremonial part of the temple service seems to have covered over and rendered obscure that which was of vital importance. There were laws many and commandments many, but tradition had turned men aside from the most obvious moral duties. "Why," said Jesus to the scribes and Pharisees, "Why do ye also transgress the commandment of God for the sake of your tradition? For God commanded, saying, Honour thy father and mother, and he that revileth father or mother let him die. But ye say, Whosoever shall say to father or mother, That (property) by which thou mightest have been helped by me is a gift to God, need not honour (*i.e.*, help) his father or mother. And ye let him do no more for father or mother, setting aside the word of God for your traditions, which ye have delivered, and many such things do ye." The priests and scribes, indeed, stood between the people and their heavenly King; and while neglecting their own duties as men, robbed the poor temporally and spiritually. "Beware of the scribes," said Jesus, "who desire to walk in long robes and to have salutations in the market places, and chief seats in the synagogues, and chief places at feasts; they who devour widows' houses, and for pretence make long prayers." Nay, not only so, but we are even told that the priest and Levite, unmoved by the commonest feelings of humanity, left the despised Samaritan to bind up wounds and care for him who fell among thieves. And thus while the priests and the priestly caste—the universal enemies of liberty and light, of justice and love—put their feet on the necks of the people, who groaned under burdens too grievous to be borne, many began to feel almost as if the heavenly Father had deserted them. The poor were in despair, and seemed to fear that God, the righteous Judge, no longer ruled among the children of men.

But Jesus, braced by the freer air of the northern country, where, apart from the deadening influence of the priests, He had communed with His own heart, with nature, and with God,—Jesus, the Prophet of Nazareth, came forth as the champion of the people. He, therefore, set His face against all this oppression by scribe and Pharisee and priest, and endeavoured to reassure His fellow-men of the fact that, in spite of all the evils which they so plainly saw around them, and from which they so manifestly suffered, this world is none the less subject to the righteous rule of God, Who is not only the King, but the Father of all mankind. We read in the Second Gospel, "Now, after John was delivered up, Jesus came into Galilee, preaching the Gospel of God, and saying, The time is fulfilled, and the kingdom of God is at hand; repent ye and believe the good news." Here, then, is the first doctrine which Jesus preached; and here, in His own words, we find what constitutes the gospel which He delivered to man,—the gospel of God. The Prophet of Nazareth bade the oppressed, the downtrodden, the sorrowful, and the sinful, take heart, because God rules among men; and, therefore, though evil may endure for a season, " the wrong shall fail, the right prevail." Jesus seems to have desired that men should see " the whole world burning with Deity."

So important did Jesus think this gospel message, that it is found, not only in His first public address, but it occurs in the Sermon on the Mount over and over again. The Beatitudes begin with it: " Blessed are the poor in spirit, for theirs is the kingdom of heaven." And not only so, but we find it in the only prayer which He gave to His disciples, " Thy kingdom come." Aye, so important did He think it was that men should enter the kingdom, that He says, "Seek ye first His kingdom and His righteousness." Jesus tells us, too, who shall enter the kingdom, " Not every one that saith unto Me, Lord, Lord; but he that doeth the will of My Father Who is in heaven." And again, " Whosoever shall not receive the kingdom of God as a little child shall in no wise enter therein." We read, indeed, that this Prophet went about all the cities and villages, " preaching the gospel of the kingdom." So, likewise, when He sent forth His twelve disciples, He commanded them, " As ye go, preach, saying, The kingdom of heaven is at hand." In fact, the heart and soul and mind of Jesus, with all their strength, were given up to this message concerning the kingdom of God; He was full of the gospel. We are told, "Without a parable spake He not to the people;" and, if we look through the parables, we find they, like the rest of His teaching, are pervaded by the same thought, that God rules among the children of men.

But even this special doctrine of the prophets Jesus modified and improved. First of all, He did away with the political feeling connected with the idea of a kingdom of God; and then He transformed the thought which was underlying the whole conception. It was not to be a kingdom of this world, although it was to be a kingdom in this world. It was to be heavenly, but it was none the less to be on the earth. Hence the disciples were to pray, as of old, "Thy kingdom come;" but they were also to pray, "Thy will be done on earth, as it is in heaven." Being asked by the Pharisees when the kingdom of God cometh, He answered, "The kingdom of God cometh not with observation; neither shall they say, Lo, here! or there! For lo, the kingdom of God is within you." And not only so; but this Prophet from Nazareth further taught that the heavenly King is "Our Father." We see this in the prayer which He gave to His disciples. Moreover, when little children were brought to Him that He might bless them, He said, "Of such is the kingdom of God. Verily I say unto you, Whosoever shall not receive the kingdom of God as a little child, he shall in no wise enter therein." In this way Jesus taught that He Who had been called a King in Israel was "Our Father;" and, *therefore*, that we, who are His subjects, must be not only in word, but in deed, His children. The rule of God is that of a father; and, *therefore*, our obedience must be that of children.

Thus the Prophet of Nazareth proclaimed a doctrine which was to bring down heaven to earth, and so help and bless toiling, suffering, and sinful man. For the kingdom of God is a kingdom of righteousness. "Seek ye first His kingdom and His righteousness;" for, " except your righteousness shall exceed the righteousness of the scribes and Pharisees, ye shall in no case enter the kingdom of heaven." And it is true, in spite of all the evil we see around us—aye, and in spite of all the evil we find in our own hearts,—it is true that God rules on earth as He rules in heaven; for ever, and always, does He rule in righteousness. "Earth's crammed with Heaven, and every common bush afire with God." Man never can do wrong, and then feel fully and truly happy. It is alone by being faithful and true, that he gains genuine peace. And who makes it so but God? And God never deceives; never does He make false promises, or keep back the reward of well-doing. Verily God rules; for He Who is wise and good directs the path of the just. And, therefore, it is the good, and not the bad, the wise, and not the foolish, who best follow the laws of their being. But why is it so, unless it be that these laws are the laws of God? But they are the laws of God; for, in the long run, all through history, is it true—true in the life of the individual as it is true in the life of nations—true now, as in the past, that

> "Ever the right comes uppermost,
> Ever is justice done."

There's a Divinity doth shape our ends, rough-hew them how we may. In the outer world, as we see, evolution is the law of growth. So, too, in the history of the race we see the same law of progression. But this rule has its exceptions. Both plants and animals may retrograde, until their last state becomes worse than their former. It is so with nations; it is so with individuals. Where are the universal monarchies that once dominated this earth? The empire of Cyrus is broken up, and its power departed. Greece, whose thought once ruled even her conquerors, has shrunk into a minor state. Rome, the once proud mistress of the world, after centuries of weakness, is but struggling once again into the light of life. Where, too, are all the old civilisations? The New World is not new, but is the tomb of former generations whose history has died unsung. But look at the Old World. The great Empire of China possesses an arrested civilisation. The Jews, as a nation, are scattered to the four winds. Egypt is rotten to the very core. Phœnicia is no more. Troy, Babylon, Carthage, are each a heap of ruins. And He Who rules the nations also rules in the hearts of individual men. He that persistently chooses evil, and not good, will and must come to grief. There is no strength in man apart from righteousness. The kingdom of God is a rule of right; and man, if he would truly live, must be holy, for God is holy. Sin ever leads to death.

> "Though the mills of God grind slowly, yet they grind exceeding small;
> Though with patience He stands waiting, with exactness grinds He all."

CHAPTER V.

THE COMMANDMENTS OF JESUS.

It is indeed strange that it should still be necessary, in this nineteenth century, to ask, What are the essential elements of the Christian religion? But this question is still pressing upon us for solution, and perhaps now more than ever needs an answer. Year after year, month after month, week after week, the literature of the Churches increases; and yet we remain as far off as ever from any satisfactory solution of this apparently easy though important question. And, therefore, instead of meeting on ground where all good men might unite for noble work, the professed followers of Jesus are ranging themselves under an ever-increasing number of banners, often wasting their resources, and vainly consuming their strength, while their common enemies— ignorance, selfishness, and sin,—lie not only around them, but even in the very heart of their own camps. No; men are not yet agreed as to what are the first principles of the religion of Jesus. More than eighteen centuries have passed away since the death of the great Prophet of Nazareth, but the Christian Churches have not solved this important problem; they have not told men, in clear and decisive language, what Christianity really is. And why is it even so? It is because the Churches prefer the obscure to the simple; because they have gone for their theology to Paul, who never saw the Master in the flesh, instead of going to the teaching of Jesus Himself, Whom in word they acknowledge to be the Founder of their faith. I remember once finding myself as a worshipper in a small country church on the thirteenth Sunday after Trinity, when the clergyman read, as the Gospel of the day, that passage in the tenth chapter of Luke wherein a certain lawyer asks the Master, "What shall I do to inherit eternal life?" And when it came to the sermon, the minister, although he preached on eternal life, not only left the Gospel for the day and selected his text from the Epistle (Paul's Epistle to the Galatians), but he commenced his address in the following words, "My friends, there are two ways of getting to heaven: there is the way marked out by Jesus Christ in the Gospel for the day, but that is no good; then there is the way marked out by St. Paul in our text, and that is the road we must take." Nothing, moreover, is more certain than the fact that not simply here and there has a teacher preferred the doctrines of Paul to the words of Jesus, but all through the history of Christendom the various sects, with hardly an exception, have made the same vital mistake. And thus has it come to pass that the Churches, while professing to be Christian, have to a great extent ignored the plainest teaching of Jesus, whilst they have substituted for His simple and glorious gospel doctrines hard to be believed, —yea, doctrines which, if ever so fully believed, have no beneficial effect on life and conduct.

I admit that, in tracing the history and development of the Churches, it might be well to consult the epistles of Paul before we examined the records contained in the Gospels; for these epistles contain the earliest written accounts of that great social and religious movement which eventually revolutionised the world. But it does not follow, from this admission, that it is well to go to Paul, instead of going to Jesus, if our desire is to know what are the essential elements of Christianity itself. Inasmuch as Paul wrote his epistles before the Gospels were composed, it may be wise to refer to his teaching, in order to see how far it may have influenced the records of the Evangelists. But, since Paul had no personal knowledge of Jesus, what right have the Churches for assuming that he necessarily interpreted correctly the mind of his Master? Happily, however, it is not necessary to enter here upon this difficult subject; and I desire, as far as possible, to avoid all questions of a controversial character. But it is surely safe to say, Either Paul's teaching does, or it does not, agree with the spirit of the teaching of the great Prophet. If it does this, even then it would still be possible to find out what was the message of Jesus from the Gospels themselves. But, if the spirit of Paul's teaching does not agree with the spirit of the teaching of the great Prophet, then most certainly it would be well to seek for a truer Christianity than he presents us with in the teaching of Jesus. It must, therefore, be safer and better, from every point of view, to go to Jesus, rather than to Paul, for our Christianity.

Not only, however, have the Churches founded their views of religion on the writings of Paul far more than on the words of Jesus, but, as a result of this mistake, they have committed another error. For they have often placed thought and opinion before fidelity to conviction and purity of life; yea, they have even taught that what they consider true opinions are necessary for man's salvation. Yet, most assuredly, the essence of religion, as taught by Jesus in the Gospels, is not opinion, but love. This Galilean Prophet tells us the first great commandment is, "The Lord our God, the Lord is one; and thou shalt *love* the Lord thy God with all thy heart, and with all thy soul, and with all thy mind." And He adds, "The second is like unto it, Thou shalt *love* thy neighbour as thyself." He even says, "On these two commandments hang all the law and the prophets." And, in another place, we read, "By this shall all men know that ye are My disciples, if ye have love one to another." Here, then, we find "the centre in the innermost shrine of Christianity." Oh, that the Churches had seen this, that they might have bound together all the children of men in one brotherhood all the world over! But the Churches have been blind to this great fact, and therefore it was that Abraham Lincoln once said, "When any Church will inscribe over its altar as its sole qualification for membership the Saviour's condensed statement of the substance of both law and gospel in those two great commandments, that Church will I join with all my heart, and with all my soul." And hence Dean Stanley, remarking on this statement, said, "If any Church existed which in reality and in spirit put forth these two commandments as the sum and substance of its belief, as that to which all else tended, and for the sake of which all was done, it would, indeed, take the first place among the Churches of the world, because it would be the Church that most fully had expressed the mind and intention of the Founder of Christendom."* And yet, as the good Dean elsewhere only too truly remarks, " in the history of the Christian Church, and of Christian theology, the moral and practical parts have been, with almost one consent, regarded as not of primary, but of secondary importance. In creeds the moral attributes of God are scarcely mentioned; the practical aspects of Christ's life are hardly thought worth a passing notice. In the Bible the passages which relate to the moral character of God and the moral duty of man have been set aside as mere subordinate and accidental parts of religion. The two commandments of Christ have been rejected

* "Christian Institutions."

as not deserving to be ranked as part of the catholic faith." This is, indeed, a grave indictment to bring against the professed disciples of Jesus; and yet how true! But grieved as I am to find that the Christian Church has strayed so often, and so far, from the Master's teaching, I rejoice to find that some at least are resolved to retrace the false steps of the ages, and to plead for the rightful place of those undying principles and truths which were inculcated by the great Prophet of the first century. I rejoice that many thoughtful and pure-minded men and women are coming to see and acknowledge, that life and character, and the real Christian spirit of the mind and heart, are far more important than the acceptance of creeds or articles of religion. For love and reverence and trust are the true elements of religion; and, compared with these, all else is mere accessory. The one thing needful is to have the heart right, as in the sight of God, our heavenly Father, Whose name and essence is love; and whatever destroys or lessens this love in the hearts of His children is Anti-Christ. And, therefore, as the ages roll on, I pray that the number may ever increase of those who seek to build alone on that foundation which Jesus Himself laid,—love to God, and love to man. For, without love, who can know anything either of the Fatherhood of God, or of the brotherhood of man? But, with love, may not every one hope to possess the sum and substance, the root and branch of true Christianity?

For what else can be more fundamental, more necessary, than this simple and grand element of religion? What else in the teaching of Jesus takes a more unique position than love? Wherever, then, we find a man who really loves God and his neighbour, we are bound to acknowledge him as a Christian; for, whatever may be his profession of religion, or want of profession, he shows by his life that he has accepted the Christian commandments. And, since these two commandments are the only commandments which Jesus gave to His disciples (for the new commandment, "that ye love one another," is identical with the second of these two), we must conclude that in them, and in them alone, lies the heart and soul of that form of religion which He taught.

It is well known, moreover, that there are no parts of the synoptic Gospels which are more reliable than those which report the words of Jesus; and, surely, where His words are reported with only slight variations, both in the First and in the Second and in the Third Gospel, we may be doubly and trebly sure that we are actually dealing with His own teaching. It so happens that many of the parables are related by one evangelist alone, and some of them may be open to more than a single interpretation. But the Christian commandments, in sum and substance, occur in each of the three synoptic Gospels, and their principle of love runs through the whole teaching of Jesus, and is ever illustrated in His life both by deeds as well as words. Nothing is more plain and unequivocal than the message of the Prophet of Nazareth contained in His two great commandments; and the position which He assigns to them is unique, since He affirms, "There is none other commandment greater than these," and still further adds, "On these two commandments hang all the law and the prophets."

Who, then, can doubt that, if Jesus taught anything, He taught love to God and love to man? And, if one principle is more fundamental than any other in His teaching, who can doubt that this principle is love? Furthermore, who can doubt that, if any part of His teaching is more important, more typical than any other part, it is precisely these two commandments? Yet, throughout eighteen centuries of their history, the Churches have gradually left these commandments in the background, and, instead of insisting on their acceptance as the bond of Christian fellowship, have much rather insisted on belief in creeds and articles and cardinal points, as though they were the vital elements of the Christian faith! Many, very many, professing and calling themselves Christians, have sought for their religion only too frequently in works of theology bristling with technicalities and fine-drawn metaphysical distinctions! Many, too, have clung to a creed full of incomprehensibles! And why has it been so in the past? Why is it still so in the present? It is because Christendom has preferred the obscurity of Paul to the simplicity of Jesus. Nay, the Churches have not even been content to accept the words of Paul as they stand in their context, but, taking a passage of his teaching here and a passage there, they have evolved their own conclusions from them by a process of reasoning; and then have thrust these conclusions upon the hearts and consciences of men as the true and only religion of the Christ. But is not this method, even if it did ultimately lead to the truth, a most roundabout and uncertain method of arriving at the religion of Jesus? Would it not be better to go to the great Prophet Himself? Would it not be a simpler way of knowing what He taught if men went straight to His words, instead of receiving His message second or third-hand as it comes through the medium of the Churches or even of the apostle of the Gentiles? Why see through a glass darkly where we may see face to face? Already are many freely saying, they cannot believe all they hear at church or chapel. To-day not more than half of our population attend any place of worship at all; and of those who do conform to the outward forms of religion how many observe its rites and ceremonies simply because it is considered respectable to do so! Or, again, how often do we hear it said, Well, I attend church, because I wish to set a good example! Can this state of things last for ever? Will we, then, not learn a lesson from our neighbours across the Channel before it is too late? Will we take no warning until in England, too, as in so many Continental countries, the churches become deserted by the educated and thoughtful, as well as by the great masses of our people. I am persuaded that, if our

Churches would win back the poor whom they have now lost, if they would keep in their possession what is still left to them of the intellect of the nation, they must insist on the fewest, the simplest, the grandest principles and truths bequeathed to them by the Master as alone essential for the acceptance of their children. They must proclaim, with one voice, the great fact insisted on by the Prophet of Nazareth, that religion may be summed up in love—love to God and love to man.

> "The uplifted eye, the bended knee,
> Are but vain homage, Lord, to Thee;
> In vain our lips Thy praise prolong,
> The heart a stranger to the song.
>
> "'Love God and man,'—that great command
> Doth on eternal pillars stand;
> This did Thy ancient prophets teach,
> And this Thy Well-Beloved preach.".

CHAPTER VI.

THE FATHERHOOD OF GOD.

I HAVE said that, so far as we can gather from the life of Jesus, He never separated Himself from the communion of Israel, or sought to establish any new form of faith. But, although the doctrines of Jesus were the doctrines of Judaism, that is, of the Jewish *prophets*, yet He laid special stress on some particular parts of their teaching. I have pointed out that the first proclamation which the Prophet of Nazareth made was the good news that the kingdom of God was near to the children of men, and that this gospel was ever present in His mind and heart, and became the foundation of all His subsequent teaching. In "filling out" this thought of the earlier prophets of His people there was, however, another doctrine upon which He soon learned to dwell with all the force of His loving character, for to the mind of Jesus it was not alone enough that God should be a King to His people collectively, He must also become a Father to each individual soul.

But how far can we say that even this doctrine of the Fatherhood of God is new? To what extent can it be said to have grown out of the earlier teaching of psalmist and prophet? The older Hebrews had certainly learned to look upon Jehovah as a Father as well as a King. In Deuteronomy (viii. 5) we read, "As a man chasteneth his son, so the Lord thy God chasteneth thee." And in 1 Chronicles (xxix. 10) we further read, "Blessed be Thou, Lord God of Israel, our Father, for ever and ever." Nor is it different in the Psalms. For in Psalm lxviii. 5 we find the words, "A Father to the fatherless and a Judge of the widows is God in His holy habitation." And in Psalm lxxxii. 6, "I have said, ye are gods, and all of you are children of the Most High." And again, in Psalm ciii. 13, "Like as a father pitieth his children, so the Lord pitieth them that fear Him." In Proverbs, too (iii. 12), we read, "For whom the Lord loveth He correcteth, even as a father the son in whom he delighteth." The same doctrine, as we should expect, runs through the Prophets. Isaiah (lxiii. 16) says, "Doubtless Thou art our Father though Abraham be ignorant of us and Israel acknowledge us not; Thou, O Lord, art our Father, our Redeemer; Thy name is from everlasting." And in another place (lxiv. 8), "But now, O Lord, Thou art our Father; we are the clay, and Thou our potter, and we are the work of Thy hand." In Jeremiah, too (xxxi. 9), we have the words, "I am a Father to Israel, and Ephraim is My first-born." In Hosea (i. 10) we read concerning Israel, "Ye are the sons of the living God." And in Malachi (ii. 10), "Have we not all one Father? Hath not one God created us?"

But does any one of all these glorious utterances of the olden Scriptures do more than teach that as God was first regarded as a King in Israel, so subsequently He was looked upon as a Father to the people, taken collectively as a corporate body? If we examine even that passage from the later Isaiah, "Doubtless Thou art our Father, though Abraham be ignorant of us, and Israel acknowledge us not; Thou, O Lord, art our Father, our Redeemer; Thy name is from everlasting," what do we find that it teaches? At first sight it may to some perhaps seem to refer to the Gentiles, but is it not far more probable, as Samuel Sharpe* points out, "that this was written by one of those whom the haughty descendants of the captives said were not Jews but strangers"? Is not the whole passage, indeed, written in the interest of those who regarded themselves as of the Israel of God, though their right was disputed by other sections of the community? Can the words, by any possible interpretation, be made to include the Gentiles as among the children of God? No; this larger hope is excluded, for immediately after this noble burst of faith we read, "O Lord, why hast Thou made us to err from Thy ways, and hardened our hearts from Thy fear? Return for Thy servants' sake, the tribes of Thine inheritance. The people of Thy holiness have possessed it" (Thine inheritance) "but a little while; our adversaries have trodden down Thy sanctuary. We

---

* "The Book of Isaiah." By Samuel Sharpe.

are Thine;" (but) "Thou never barest rule over them; they were never called by Thy name."

It is no doubt true that the prophets did look forward to a future period, when all the nations of the earth should bow down before the Lord, and worship Him as the one only true God; but even then the Gentiles were not to enter within the covenanted mercies of Jehovah on equal terms with the children of Israel. Not even the "Gospel prophet," as the later Isaiah has been called, gives expression to the thought that all men are equally sons of the Most High. He does say (lx. 1-3), "Arise, shine, for thy light is come, and the glory of the Lord is risen upon thee. For, behold, the darkness shall cover the earth, and gross darkness the people; but the Lord shall arise upon thee, and His glory shall be seen upon thee. And the Gentiles shall come to thy light, and kings to the brightness of thy rising." But how were the nations to come to the light? Not as the equals of Israel, not as their brethren, but rather as their slaves. As we read in another passage of the same great prophet (xlix. 22-3), "Thus saith the Lord God, I will lift up Mine hand to the Gentiles and set up My standard to the people, and they shall bring thy sons in their arms, and thy daughters shall be carried upon their shoulders. And kings shall be thy nursing fathers, and their queens thy nursing mothers; they shall bow down to thee with their faces toward the earth, and lick up the dust of thy feet." Nor is it going too far to assert that the middle wall of partition between Gentile and Jew was never broken down in pre-Christian times, for, right up to the days of Jesus, to pass the limits allowed to the heathen in the temple was to them instant death. The fact is, that before the time of the Prophet of Nazareth God was regarded, even in Israel, simply as a Father to the collective people, and not as the parent of each individual man. And, as F. W. Newman truly remarks, "All ancient nations, Gentile and Hebrew, accounted it a rightful function of the civil power to dictate religion to the community. The deep-thinking Aristotle agreed herein with received Mosaic doctrine."* And, as we have already seen, he further says: "Antiquity certainly had not learned that private men had any right to a conscience. The main reason was this, religion in their idea was essentially external and corporate, not individual, personal, internal, as Jesus in every utterance assumes it to be. He never dilates on the covenant of Jehovah with a collective Israel, but dwells on the relation of each separate worshipper to the Father in heaven as a private affair. This was the fruitful germ, this was the 'seed of mustard,' by which He virtually called His countrymen to free thinking concerning their national institutions." And may I not add that it was precisely this personal relation between each individual soul and the great Parent Spirit, which was the foundation of the doctrine of the Fatherhood of God as taught by Jesus? We see, then, that it was

* "Christianity in its Cradle." By F. W. Newman.

reserved for the Prophet of Nazareth to place this glorious doctrine on that basis where alone it can embrace all men of every clime and creed—aye, and of no creed,—in one universal brotherhood. And not only did Jesus dwell upon this doctrine of God's Fatherhood more than all His forerunners put together, but in His hands it assumed a fuller form and a deeper meaning. He so proclaimed it as to embrace the whole human family, and yet, at the same time, in such a way as to lead each individual, without priest or mediator, into direct personal relation with the Father of us all.

The teaching of Jesus, moreover, is full of this all-embracing doctrine. When His disciples asked Him to teach them how to pray, Jesus said unto them, "When ye pray, say, Father, hallowed be Thy name." So, again, in the Sermon on the Mount, we read, "Behold the birds of the heaven, that they sow not, neither do they reap, nor gather into barns; and your heavenly Father feedeth them. Are ye not of much more value than they?" In time of trouble, too, Jesus said that His disciples were not to be anxious how, or what, they should speak : "For it is not ye that speak, but the Spirit of your Father." Aye, He told them, "Not a sparrow shall fall to the ground without your Father." "Fear not, therefore," He added; "ye are of more value than many sparrows." And, comparing the love and care of an earthly father with the love and care of the heavenly Father, He said, "If ye, then, being evil, know how to give good gifts unto your children, how much more shall your heavenly Father give a holy spirit to them that ask Him?"

We find, too, that the Galilean Prophet always refers to God as His Father, as well as our Father. "Not every one that saith unto Me, Lord! Lord! shall enter into the kingdom of heaven; but he that doeth the will of My Father, which is in heaven." So, also, in His deepest hour of need, He cried: "O My Father, if it be possible, let this cup pass away from Me; nevertheless, not as I will, but as Thou wilt." And, again, we read, "Father, into Thy hands I commend My Spirit."

In this doctrine of the Fatherhood of God as taught by Jesus, there is, moreover, a tone and spirit not found in the teaching of earlier days. According to the Prophet of Nazareth, men are not to be the sons of God in the deepest and truest sense because they are the children of Abraham, nor because they have been baptized, but because of some Divine quality in themselves. "Blessed are the peacemakers; for they shall be called the sons of God." Hence we read, "Ye have heard that it was said, Thou shalt love thy neighbour, and hate thine enemy; but I say unto you, Love your enemies, and pray for them that persecute you; that ye may be sons of your Father, which is in heaven; for He maketh His sun to rise on the evil and the good, and sendeth rain on the just and the unjust." "Be ye therefore perfect, since your heavenly Father is perfect."

And how much is included in this doctrine as

developed in the teaching of Jesus! Behold how merciful is God represented as being in the parable of the prodigal, both in His dealings with the elder as well as with the younger son! There is no hint in this parable, any more than in any other part of the teaching of this great Prophet, there is no slightest word, no least syllable concerning the "satisfaction of justice," or about a "mediator," or the barest reference to the doctrine of Christ being either a "Priest" or a "Sacrifice." Not that Jesus ever led men to suppose that because God is merciful, sin will ever escape its just penalty. As Mozley, in his Oxford "Reminiscences," observes, "All sin is irreparable, any act of sin whatever. It leaves its consequences on heart, mind, body, and soul, on those who share it, and on those who suffer from it. This is a truth, not of revelation, but of natural fact." And why is it so but because God, "Our Father," is just, and wise, and good; and because these various words, by which we describe His character, are only so many different names for that one absolute and Divine quality, which we regard as perfect in Him Who is perfection? For, because God is one and perfect, His justice is His mercy; and both His justice and His mercy are equally His goodness and His wisdom and His love. This, too, is why error ever brings evil in its train, and every sin its punishment, even as every rightness is followed by its fit reward.

Thus, in the poetical language of the East, we read, that when the young man in the parable had spent all, "there arose a mighty famine in that country; and he began to be in want." Nay, more; for it was this very "want" which led to his repentance; and, when he came to himself, he said, "I will arise and go to my father."

> "Not Thou from us, O Lord, but we
>   Withdraw ourselves from Thee.
>   When we are dark and dead,
> And Thou art covered with a cloud,
> Hanging about Thee like a shroud,
> So that our prayer can find no way,
> O teach us that we do not say,
>   'Where is *Thy* brightness fled?'
>   But that we search and try
> What in ourselves has wrought this blame:
> For Thou remainest still the same;
> But earth's own vapours earth may fill
> With darkness and thick clouds, while still
>   The sun is in the sky."

Verily, verily is sin a departure from God, a dwelling in a far-off country, where we live apart from love, and far from home. And by the justice and the mercy and the love and the goodness of God, we can find no peace in sin; for peace, like holiness, is of God, and is only shared in by us as we draw near to God, and become somewhat like Him. Then, and only then, are we in the fullest sense of the word children of our Father; then, and only then, do we dwell in Him, and He in us; then, and only then, can we say, "I and my Father are one."

But then, if only then, the justice of God tends to

make His children just, even as His mercy tends to make them merciful, His goodness to make them good, His wisdom to make them wise, and His love to make them lovely. And it is because all these truths are involved in this doctrine of the Fatherhood of God, as taught by the Prophet from Nazareth,—I say, it is *because* of this, that Jesus said, "Ye, therefore, shall be perfect, since your heavenly Father is perfect."

Yes, the Prophet of Nazareth was the first to teach this fuller doctrine so plainly and so emphatically, and to show that it involves such complete likeness between parent and child; and never before was the Fatherhood of God ever exhibited in so exquisite a form. In the parable of the Prodigal we see the long-forbearing and generous love of God so painted, that all must understand and admire. The elder son is made to speak of the younger, when addressing their common father, as "thy son;" and, in his self-righteousness, he boasts of his own long service, and complains of what he deems its want of recognition. But the father says, it was meet to make merry, and be glad; for this "thy brother" was dead, and is alive again; and was lost, and is found. So, too, the father watches for the return of the prodigal; and not only does he see him while he is yet afar off, not only is he moved with compassion, but he runs and falls on his neck, and kisses him. And, moreover, when the elder son is angry, and will not go in to meet his brother, the father comes out and entreats him. Surely, then, this doctrine of the Fatherhood of God was never taught so fully, nor with such matchless grace, before the time of Jesus. It was the great Prophet of Nazareth Who first represented God, not simply as the Creator, or King, or Father of a chosen people, to the exclusion of the other nations of the earth, but as the Father of man as man. It is, therefore, this Prophet Who has led men to love God as He was never loved before. Jesus founded no Church. He never, so far as we know, sought to found a Church; His object was to form a family. And if ever men learn to live on this earth like brethren, and come to see that they have but one Father, I believe they will also, and at the same time, come to feel that they were led to this great consummation through the message of the outcast Nazarene.

> "Father, gracious Father!
>   God of might and power!
> Thou Thyself art dwelling
>   In us at this hour.
>
> Yea, the hearts of children
>   Hold what worlds cannot;
> And the God of wonders
>   Loves the lowly spot.
>
> Father, gracious Father!
>   Thou art in us now;
> Fill us full of goodness,
>   Till our hearts o'erflow."

CHAPTER VII.

THE BROTHERHOOD OF MAN.

IN the explorations of the Jewish Temple of Jerusalem one of the stones has been discovered which belonged to the barrier that separated the court of the Israelites from the court of the Gentiles; and on this stone was found the inscription in Greek, still legible, forbidding all Gentiles under pain of death to pass beyond their allotted place. To the Jews, therefore, the terms "brother" and "neighbour" could hardly have included the Gentiles. And not only does this fact seem to be made clear by this incription, which formed a part of the Temple itself; but, if we search through the Hebrew scriptures, we find that the words "neighbour" and "brother" and "brethren" refer alone to those who were kith and kin with Israel. In Nehemiah (v. 8) we read, "We after our ability have redeemed our brethren the Jews." It is the same even in the writings of the prophets. Jeremiah (xxxi. 33-4) says "But this shall be the covenant that I will make with the house of Israel: After these days, saith the Lord I will put My law in their inward parts, and write it in their hearts; and I will be their God, and they shall be My people. And they shall no more teach every man his neighbour, and every man his brother, saying, Know ye the Lord; for they shall all know Me, from the least of them unto the greatest of them, saith the Lord." Ezekiel, too, writes (xxxiii. 30), "Also, thou son of man, the children of thy people still are talking against thee by the walls, and in the doors of the houses, and speak one to another, every man to his brother." Thus it is all through the Hebrew scriptures; for always, and everywhere, they make all three terms, "neighbour," "brother," and "brethren," refer exclusively to the people of Israel.

It is perfectly true that the utmost kindness, and the most thoughtful care, were to be freely bestowed upon every member of this one community by each and all within its borders. The poor especially were to be regarded with fraternal love; but this goodwill was to be limited to one's "neighbours" within the single race of Israel. In Leviticus (xix. 17, 18) we read, "Thou shalt not hate thy brethren in thine heart; thou shalt in any wise rebuke thy neighbour, and not suffer sin upon him. Thou shalt not avenge, nor bear any grudge against the children of thy people; but shalt love thy neighbour as thyself." And again (xxv. 35), we further read, "If thy brother be waxen poor, and fallen in decay with thee, then thou shalt relieve him." There is the same kindly feeling inculcated in Deuteronomy (xv. 11), "Thou shalt open thine hand wide unto thy brother, to thy poor, and to thy needy, in thy land. And, if thy brother, a Hebrew man or a Hebrew woman, be sold unto thee, and serve thee six years; then, on the seventh year, thou shalt let him go free from thee." A similar injunction is likewise found in the prophet Jeremiah (xxxiv. 8, 9), "This is the word which came unto Jeremiah from the Lord, after that the king Zedekiah had made a covenant with all the people which were at Jerusalem, to proclaim liberty unto them; that every man should let his manservant, and every man his maidservant, being a Hebrew, or a Hebrewess, go free; that none should serve himself of them, to wit, of a Jew his brother." The Jews, moreover, have ever acted up to their own laws and commandments; and, to this day, we never see a Jew begging bread. But, none the less, while we find the most scrupulous care exercised for the people of their own race, the terms "neighbour" and "brother" are certainly confined in their own scriptures to the Hebrews alone.

There are, however, a few apparent exceptions to this rule. In Deuteronomy (xxiii. 7) we find the words, "Thou shalt not abhor an Edomite, for he is thy brother; thou shalt not abhor an Egyptian, because thou wast a stranger in his land." But these exceptions only prove the rule. For though we read, "Edom is thy brother," yet the name "Edom" stands for "Esau," the firstborn son of Isaac, and brother, therefore, of Jacob or Israel. Even Egypt is not here called a "brother" or a "neighbour" to Israel, but all we are told is, that, because she saved the Hebrews in a time of famine, therefore Egypt is not to be abhorred. But the mere fact that these two peoples—the one because related by blood to the Hebrews, the other because of services rendered to them in time of distress—were thus singled out from all the other nations of the earth, "Thou shalt not *abhor* an Edomite," "Thou shalt not *abhor* an Egyptian," only shows but too plainly how Israel generally regarded the Gentiles; and it also fully justifies the words of Jesus, "Ye have heard that it hath been said, Thou shalt love thy neighbour, but hate thine enemy."

I am aware that in Exodus (xxiii. 4, 5) we read, "If thou meet thine *enemy's* ox or his ass going astray, thou shalt surely bring it back to him again. If thou see the ass of him that *hateth* thee lying under his burden, and wouldest forbear to help him, thou shalt surely help with him." But, is it not fair to assume that here the word "enemy," as well as the phrase "him that hateth thee," both refer, if not to Hebrews, at least to people within the borders of Israel? For in Leviticus (xix. 34) we read, "And if a stranger sojourn with thee in your land, ye shall not do him wrong. The stranger that sojourneth with you shall be unto you as the homeborn among you, and thou shalt love him as thyself; for ye were strangers in the land of Egypt." And this teaching of Leviticus is confirmed in the second law; for we read in Deuteronomy (x. 19), "Love ye therefore the stranger; for ye were strangers in the land of Egypt." Although, then, we see that the children of Israel were not to be less kind to other peoples than other peoples had been to them, I think we find no evidence that the Hebrews before the time of Jesus had arrived at the thought, that all nations formed but one family,—a brotherhood of man.

We are now, perhaps, in a position to see how great a revolution the Prophet of Nazareth wrought in the religion of His countrymen by the deeper meaning which He put into the word "neighbour." Among so-called "savage" races the tribe forms a kind of unit in society. The members of each tribe, therefore, are bound together by a community of thought and feeling. Hence, in the time of war (and early man was always at war) every man was bound to protect his "neighbour" or fellow-tribesman equally with himself. And thus within the tribe we frequently find the most scrupulous honesty, and a large amount of mutual helpfulness. Max Müller, in an article on "The Savage,"* speaking of the Iroquois Indians, who are often referred to as specimens of extreme savagery, quotes an American scholar, Mr. Morgan, as saying of these people, "No test of friendship was too severe, no sacrifice to repay a favour too great, no fidelity to an engagement too inflexible for a red man. With an innate knowledge of the freedom and dignity of man, he has exhibited the noblest virtues of the heart, and the kindest deeds of humanity, in those sylvan retreats we are wont to look upon as vacant and frightful solitudes." But fre-

* *Nineteenth Century*, January 1885.

quently, as if to compensate for the great care for each other's welfare which is exhibited within the pale of the tribe, there is among uncivilised men the utmost licence in their dealings with the members of other tribes beyond their own limits. In the outer world, therefore, every man's hand is against every other man; and theft and murder become the ordinary occupation of daily life.

Among the Jews, however, we find, in Old Testament times, twelve different tribes growing into one nation. Not only, therefore, in spite of some community of interest, is one tribe frequently opposed to another tribe; but, even after a kingdom is established, it becomes divided into two parts—north and south—each with varying wants and different interests. Nevertheless the people, in some sort, feel themselves to be one; and they agree to stand together in order to maintain their peculiar institutions against all other nations. For Israel came to think they were all equally the children of Abraham, and, therefore, of one stock and blood. Thus the unity which they strove to defend was not that of a single tribe, but that of an entire people; and "neighbour" or "brother" to the Hebrews signified an Israelite, or at most it included those who dwelt within their borders. Nor was it either king or priest who enlarged the meaning of these terms; but the work was left to that Galilean Prophet, Who, near His northern home, had come in contact with the people of many lands—with settlers from Phœnicia and the Greek colonies, with

Roman officers and soldiers, and even with wanderers from the wild deserts of the East, and travellers from Syria and Arabia. Jesus did not break away from the religion of His fathers; He taught no new doctrines; He introduced no new rites; He added not one single article of belief to the faith of Israel; and yet, by the spirit which He infused into that faith, He created a revolution in religion; for He humanised and so developed and deepened the best thoughts and feelings which had been evolved in earlier times by the prophets of His people. This revolution, moreover, though so vast, was equally simple, and may almost be said to have taken its rise from the transfiguration of a single word,—the word " neighbour." The Prophet of Nazareth taught no new system of philosophy, any more than He taught a new form of religion. He introduced no fresh moral code. All He did was to insist on the worth of man, because man is a child of God. He proclaimed, not only that men of the same nation were brothers, but taught that there was but One God and Father, and, therefore, but one family of men, whether on earth or in heaven. The Jews had already *faith in God;* but this, by itself, had made them narrow and exclusive. Jesus had also *faith in man;* He, therefore, taught that His disciples must love one another and live as brethren. Indeed, this deeper feeling of brotherhood did not even fully exist *within* the limits of Israel in the days of Jesus, notwithstanding the fact that all the people regarded themselves as children of Abraham. At this time, not only were the teachers of religion among the Hebrews divided into two hostile camps—the priests and the prophets,—but there existed a still further division among them, some being Pharisees and others Sadducees. Nay, worse still, the people also were divided; for a part, and only a part, were considered to be within the covenanted mercies of Jehovah, and the rest were looked upon as outcasts. There were synagogues in every town, and almost in every village, but many of the people never entered them, nor ever went up to the Temple at Jerusalem. Some were excommunicated for real or supposed trespasses against patriotism, religion, or morality, others for being ceremonially unclean. And those who were excommunicated by the officers of the synagogue were not allowed to attend public worship. They were known as "sinners," and, among this class, of course, were the "publicans." And both "publicans" and "sinners" were classed with the heathen, and shunned as unclean. Yes, in the days of Jesus, precisely those who appear to have stood most in need of religious aid and instruction were cut off from Israel, and treated like "Gentile dogs." To take a meal with such was as great an offence as to dine with the heathen. But, said Jesus, "The whole need not a physician, but those who are sick;" and therefore did He eat with "publicans" and "sinners." But what courage must it have required to direct His mission especially to these outcasts of society! What faith He must have had in man! What love for the poor and needy! How could He have dared, without this love and faith, to choose a publican for one of those twelve disciples who were to preach the gospel of the kingdom of God? What did the people think when, in opposition to all constituted rule and authority, He cried, "I came, not to call the righteous, but sinners"? Some thought Him mad! Other some said He was a prophet. And what would the teachers in Israel think? In the Fourth Gospel (vii. 45-49) we read, "The officers, therefore, came to the chief priests and Pharisees; and they said unto them, Why did ye not bring Him? The officers answered, Never man so spake. The Pharisees, therefore, answered them, Are ye also led astray? Hath any of the rulers believed on Him, or of the Pharisees? But this multitude, which knoweth not the law, are accursed." Jesus, however, like a strong man and true, was faithful to His mission; and, heedless of the priests, gathered together those whom they called "accursed," that He might teach them to love God and man; for He regarded even these outcasts as neighbours and brethren, children of the Father. But, although Jesus was always talking about the Father, and taught that men are His children, yet He loved to call Himself, not "Son of God," but "Son of Man." He claimed only to speak as a man to man, though He spoke for God; and, therefore, He chose for Himself the prophet's name, "Son of Man." Again and again He must have cried, "The Son of Man is come to seek and to save the lost," for His work was pre-eminently for "the lost sheep of the house of Israel."

Not that He cared alone for "the house of Israel," having no thought for the Gentiles. But He took up that duty which lay nearest to hand,—the duty, too, which was most pressing. He found some of His people treated by their brethren as though they were of alien race; for the phrase, "lost sheep of the house of Israel," is only another name for those outcast Hebrews who were regarded by the Jews as heathen. It included not only those who were formally excommunicated, but all those classes of society spoken of in the Talmud as "the people of the land." If, *e.g.*, a man, either through ignorance or carelessness, had transgressed any ceremonial law, if he had associated with the heathen (and there were very many of this class in Galilee), he became a "lost sheep of the house of Israel," and ceased to receive any further instruction in Jewish doctrine, until he underwent a particular form of ceremonial purification; but if he did not care to do this, he remained an outcast from the self-styled Israel of God. Among these "people of the land" many were on a low moral level, others again desired to know what was good and true; but they were all classed as "sinners." The professional teachers of religion regarded them as all alike unclean, and took no trouble on their behalf, and cared nothing whether they understood either the law or the prophets. Was not Jesus, then, right in turning first of all, and most of all, to these "lost sheep of the house of Israel"? And did He not do well in approaching them when He simplified religion, and summed up both the law and the prophets in *love*—love to God, and love to man? And was it not also well that His every word and deed should grow out of His faith in man, even in the outcast? Who is our neighbour? Every man! But chiefly those who are near to us, when they stand in need. "You have heard that it has been said, "Love your neighbour, and hate your enemy; but I say unto you, Love your enemies, and pray for them that persecute you, that you may be the sons of the heavenly Father, Who makes His sun to rise on the evil and on the good, and sends His rain on the just and on the unjust."

Hence we see that Jesus, in His love for man, had regard not only for the outcast of His own race, not only for those who were beyond the borders of His own people, but even for those who had sought to crush out their liberty, and overthrow their religion. For to whom did the Prophet of Nazareth refer when He said, "Love your enemies, and pray for them that *persecute* you"? Did He not refer to the heathen? The people of Israel had formerly been taught by the priests to regard it as a duty to Jehovah to hate their enemies; and their enemies were those who did not accept the religion of the Hebrews. Hence all the Gentiles were "enemies" both of God and of His people; for do we not read in the Book of Exodus (xxiii. 22), "I will be an enemy unto thine enemies, and an adversary unto thine adversaries"? And, even in the Psalms, do we not find, "Thou shalt have all the heathen in derision;" and even, "Pour out Thy wrath upon the heathen that have not known Thee, and upon the kingdoms that have not called upon Thy name"? True, the prophet Jonah was sent on a special mission to the heathen; but the later Prophet taught that there was but One Father in heaven, One family on earth. And the marvel is, not that He was allowed a ministry of only eighteen months; but that He was permitted at all to preach, as He did, throughout the towns and villages even of Galilee. For, in His day, there certainly was not much kindly feeling shown towards the heathen; and it is little wonder that some said this Prophet, Who told His people to love, and pray for, those who had trodden down their nation, was beside Himself. In the fourth chapter of our Third Gospel we read that Jesus, when He spoke in the synagogue of His native village, told His people, that there were many widows in Israel in the days of Elijah; and unto none of them was Elijah sent, but only to Zarephath, in the land of Sidon; and there were many lepers in Israel in the time of Elisha the prophet, and none of them was cleansed, but only Naaman the Syrian. But at these kindly references to the heathen, we are told the people were so enraged that they cast Jesus forth out of the city. Well might He exclaim, "No prophet is acceptable in his own country."

But much as the Jews hated the Gentiles, they hated still more their Samaritan neighbours. Yet Jesus was bold enough to say to His people, that the humane duty, which had been neglected by their own priest and Levite, had been performed by one whom they despised; and so, when He was asked by a certain lawyer, "Master, what shall I do to inherit eternal life?" He told the story of the good Samaritan, and said, "Go, and do thou likewise."

"Abou Ben Adhem—may his tribe increase!—
Awoke one night from a deep dream of peace,
And saw amid the moonlight in his room,
Making it rich, and like a lily in bloom,
An angel writing in a book of gold;
Exceeding peace had made Ben Adhem bold,
And to the vision in the room he said,
'What writest thou?' The vision raised its head,
And with a voice made of all sweet accord,
Replied, 'The names of them that love the Lord.'
'And is mine one?' said Abou. 'Nay, not so,'
Replied the angel. Abou spoke more low,
But cheerly still, and said, 'I pray thee, then,
Write me as one who loves his fellow-men.'

The angel wrote and vanished. The next night
He came again with a great wakening light;
He showed the names whom love of God had blessed,
And lo! Ben Adhem's name led all the rest."

CHAPTER VIII.

THE LAST SUPPER.

THERE are very many questions concerning the "Last Supper" which are involved in the greatest obscurity—an obscurity which time will doubtless never be able entirely to clear away. Dean Alford, commenting on this subject, says, that Matthew is "the least exact in detail;" that Mark "partially fills up the outline;" but that Luke is both "the most detailed" and "the most exact;" and that the narrative which St. Paul gives (1 Cor. xi. 23-25) "coincides almost verbatim with that given by Luke." But he adds: "It must not be forgotten that over all three narratives extends the great difficulty of reconciling the impression, undeniably conveyed by them, that the Lord and His disciples *ate the usual Passover*, with the narrative of St. John, which not only does not sanction, but, I believe, absolutely excludes such a supposition." If, then, it be granted that the evidence of the Fourth Gospel (which all writers agree is the latest in date) cannot be accepted in opposition to earlier tradition, supported, as it is, by the concurrent testimony of the three synoptic Gospels, must we not conclude that the "Last Supper" which Jesus partook with His disciples was simply the Jewish Passover?

But let us endeavour to trace out more in detail the historical facts which underlie our present Gospel stories. If, then, as Alford thinks, Matthew is the least circumstantial and the least exact in detail, while the account in Luke, with which St. Paul coincides almost verbatim, is most detailed, will not a true historical instinct decide us in favour of the version contained in the First Gospel? For is it not a fundamental rule of New Testament criticism that the simplest accounts of any event are usually the earliest, while more elaborate narratives are almost invariably of later origin? That Luke and Paul should agree in their account of this supper is perfectly natural; for it is generally admitted that the third Evangelist was under the influence of the apostle of the Gentiles. But it is also necessary to bear in mind that neither Paul nor Luke were present with Jesus and His disciples when they met together to celebrate their last Passover; so that, at best, they could only hear what was done and said at second-hand. This remark applies also, and equally, to Mark. In the case of Luke and Paul, however, there is a still further disqualification, which might render them, to some extent, out of sympathy with the actual teaching of the Master. Jesus, so far as we know, remained a Jew to the last. On the other hand, we find that Luke was not born a Jew, and that Paul, who, although a Pharisee of the Pharisees in his earlier days, subsequently departed from the faith of his fathers. Hence it is not improbable that both of these writers might interpret any act of Jesus which was strictly Jewish in its character with more or less freedom, though with unintentional bias. Wherever, then, the evidence of Luke and Paul stands in opposition to that of Matthew, who was an actual disciple of Jesus, and came into personal contact with Him, it must be ruled out of court by a fair and impartial criticism. So also the later account of the Last Supper, contained in our Fourth Gospel, must be set aside, whenever it comes into conflict with the common tradition of the synoptics. Shall we, then, be far wrong if we follow Professor Scholten, of Leyden, and say, "Originally the Lord's Supper was simply the continuance among the Jewish Christians of the Jewish Passover, hallowed, however, by the memory of Jesus, Who Himself celebrated this feast the night before His death. Then Paul and the Pauline Evangelist, who, as anti-legalists, would have nothing to do with any celebration of the Passover, make Jesus institute the supper of the new covenant in memory of Himself, after the celebration of the Passover; while the events disappear altogether in the Fourth Gospel, according to which Jesus was already dead when the Jews ate the Passover"?

The Passover, as we all know, was the first of the three great annual festivals celebrated by the people of Israel, and was instituted to commemorate their deliverance from the bondage of Egypt. It lasted from the fourteenth to the twenty-first of the month Nisan. On the fourteenth of the month the head of the family was to kill a lamb while the sun was setting, and was to take the blood in a basin and with a sprig of hyssop sprinkle the two side-posts and the lintel of the door of the house. The lamb was to be thoroughly roasted whole, and it was expressly forbidden that it should be boiled, or that a bone should be broken. Unleavened bread and bitter herbs were to be eaten with the flesh. All were to have their loins girt, to hold a staff in their hands, and to have their shoes on their feet. They were to eat in haste, and, it would seem, they were to stand during the whole meal. If, however, the family was very small, another family might join them, and the number of the party was to be calculated as nearly as possible so that all the flesh of the lamb might be eaten; and, if any part of it was left, it was to be burned in the morning.

It is true that in the account of this feast, as narrated in the Pentateuch, there is no mention of the use of wine, while in the Gospels it is certainly spoken of in connection with the "Last Supper;" but the Mishna, a collection of traditions which forms part of the Talmud, strictly enjoins that there shall never be less than four cups of wine at the paschal meal even of the poorest Israelite. There was also in use at the Passover a service of song called the Hallel, a word contracted from Hallelujah, and meaning "Praise ye Jehovah." This service of song consisted of psalms, and the first portion was sung in the early part of the meal, and the second portion after the fourth cup of wine. There is mention, too, of a hymn sung by the disciples both in our First and in our Second Gospel. Other innovations crept into this festival which we need not notice here; but it may be added that probably all work, excepting that belonging to a few trades connected with daily life, was suspended for some hours before the evening of the fourteenth day of the month; that it was not lawful to eat any ordinary food after midday, and that none could join in its celebration who were ceremonially unclean. The Rabbinists, too, expressly state that women were permitted, though they were not commanded to partake.

Now, whatever differences there may be in our Gospel stories concerning the Last Supper, they all agree that Jesus and His disciples were gathered together at a social meal immediately before the death of the Master. But even the three earlier Evangelists all ascribe to Jesus language which sounds very remarkable to modern ears. The First Gospel says, "Take, eat; this is My body," in relation to the bread; and of the wine we read, "Drink ye all of it; for this is My blood." The Second Gospel says, "Take ye; this is My body," speaking of the bread; and speaking of the wine, "This is My blood." In the Third Gospel, too, the alteration in the words is but slight; for here also Jesus refers to the bread as "My body," and to the wine as "My blood."

Dean Alford, however, still further affirms, when commenting on Matthew xxvi., (1) "That it was demonstrably our Lord's intention to *found an ordinance* for those who should believe in Him; (2) that this *ordinance* had *some analogy with that which He and the apostles were then celebrating.*" The first of these assertions, the Dean says, "depends on the express word of the Apostle Paul ... The second is shown by the fact that what now took place was *during the celebrations of the Passover;* that the same Paul states that *Christ our Passover is sacrificed for us.*" But we must observe that both of these statements of the Dean are based solely on the words of Paul, who was not present, and not on those of a disciple who witnessed the ceremony; and that there is really no more historical evidence for the assumption that Jesus intended to found any fresh ordinance whatever, than there is for the supposition that He desired to found a new Church.

Be this, however, as it may, what can we understand by the extraordinary language which, as we have seen, has been ascribed to the Master by all three synoptic Gospels? The Catholic Church boldly takes the words "This is My body"—"This is My blood," in their literal sense. But all Protestants agree that such phrases cannot be interpreted with prosaic literalness, and they rely on the fact that the verb "to be" is often used in Hebrew and Syriac (a dialect of which Jesus spoke) to convey the sense of "to signify." Thus they maintain that the words only mean, This bread "signifies" or "represents" My body; this wine "signifies" or "represents" My blood. But do we not now know that the tradition of later days has often put words into the mouth of Jesus which He never uttered? Do we not find a whole verse added to the Lord's Prayer from a Syrian liturgy? Do we not also read at the end of our First Gospel that Jesus bids His disciples to baptize into the name of "the Father, and of the Son, and of the Holy Ghost," although in no case of baptism, mentioned subsequently in the New Testament, do we find this form of words used? Is it not, then, better to suppose that Jesus simply adhered to the Jewish method when He distributed the bread and wine to His disciples, and with them partook of His last Paschal meal?

Can we, however, at this distance of time, find out what was the great object which Jesus had in view when He gathered His disciples together in that "upper room" at the close of His ministry among them? I think we can, and that this great object was the same which ever came uppermost in His life's work. At the Jewish Passover, we must bear in mind, it was the custom of the father of the family to preside over his own household; and only, if the families were small, were two of them allowed to unite together. But Jesus cared not for mere outward forms, but only for the inner truth contained in them. And, in collecting His disciples at His Last Supper from various families, we see that He formed them into a family; for, according to Jewish rites, the disciples should have separated and eaten the Passover each with his own kith and kin. Here, then, once again do we find this Prophet breaking through mere custom for the sake of a great principle, to achieve an important end; for it was not a mere Church that He desired to found, but far rather did He seek to form a true brotherhood of man. With Jesus the thought was never absent that God is "Our Father" —the Father of all, and that all men are brethren. Hence, just before the hour of His death, He sought to set vividly before His disciples the one great truth which His life proclaimed—the Fatherhood of God, the brotherhood of man. And even if we are wrong in supposing that it was the Passover which Jesus ate with His disciples at the close of His ministry, yet, as E. B. Tylor so truly observes, "Through all grades of civilisation the ceremony of eating and drinking together binds the partakers to behave to one another as members of the same household." Then, surely, in the Last Supper the one great lesson which is set forth above all else is the fundamental doctrine of Jesus—the brotherhood of man. This doctrine we have found everywhere either implicitly or explicitly set forth in His message; and if it had not been perverted and covered over with the traditions of the ages, if from the very first century until now the Churches had accepted it in its original simplicity, it would have become the greatest spiritual power which the world has ever seen for binding together all the nations of the earth. None before Jesus had seized so tenaciously this great idea that all men, by virtue of a common Fatherhood, form but parts of one vast family. None before Jesus had seized so tenaciously the grand idea that God is a Spirit, a holy Spirit, a Spirit of faithfulness and love; and that the one duty of the children of men is to live together in unity, in the spirit of God, as a holy family, dedicated to love and fidelity. And these two great facts—the Fatherhood of God and the brotherhood of man—are both united and made one, and set forth with living power in the Last Supper.

Yet this great truth has been lost sight of, and is still concealed by the superstitions of later days. Hence many men and women care no longer to celebrate this great commemoration. Some seem afraid of the rite, as though they thought themselves unworthy to take part in it; while others, forgetting the truth set forth in it, think they have outgrown its observance. But who would not desire to remember and hold in honour that great Prophet, Who, beyond all other prophets, sought in life and in death to free the mind and heart from superstition, that men might live like brothers? And who, worthy of the name of man or woman, ought to shrink from even a solemn pledge that he or she (with God's help) will try at least to work in the spirit of Jesus, to establish that fraternal fellowship which shall yet knit together in one bond of union all races of every clime?

"There is
One great society alone on earth
The noble living and the noble dead."

CHAPTER IX.

THE RELIGION OF HUMANITY.

NOTHING is more certain than that the religion of Israel, like the religions of all other nations, was not the same in every age, but developed step by step with the growth of the people. And is it not equally clear that the prophets, and not the priests, were the prime movers in this evolution, which ultimately led up to that latest development in which Jesus "dwells on the relation of each separate worshipper to a Father in heaven as a private affair"? The priests were often on the side of the kings, while the prophets were on the side of the people; and hence, while the former cared more for the existing order of things, and placed sacrifices and offerings in the forefront of religion, the latter were more often prepared for change and growth, caring most of all for uprightness of conduct, and for fidelity in the inner heart of the individual man. Hosea, therefore, speaking in the name of Jehovah, cries, "I desire mercy and not sacrifice, the knowledge of God more than burnt offerings;" and Isaiah, too, not only says, "To what purpose is the multitude of your sacrifices unto Me?" but also, in another place, cries, "Wash you, make you clean, put away the evil of your doings from before Mine eyes: cease to do evil, learn to do well. Seek judgment, turn away the oppressor: do justice to the fatherless, defend the cause of the widow." Not only, however, do we find a radical difference in tone and spirit between the teaching of priest and prophet, but we find also two distinct classes among the prophets,—the earlier and the later. And, according to the doctrine of development, we discover, as we should expect, that the later prophets towered above the earlier prophets in the moral grandeur of their teaching. These forerunners of Jesus were men whose force of character, whose deep convictions, whose moral courage, led them to speak out their truest thoughts, touched with the deepest emotion, as they were moved by the Spirit of God. Thus, indeed, they prepared the way for Israel's chiefest Son, in Whom culminated the true prophetic spirit,—a Man Whose force of character, Whose deep convictions, Whose moral courage, has compelled the admiration and the love of the whole civilised world in all subsequent time.

But, while the prophets of all ages helped to purify religion, and to call men away from mere outward observances to the inner realities of goodness, truth, and love, it seems to have been reserved especially for the Prophet of Nazareth to *humanise* religion, and to show that the primal duty of the children of God is to serve and help and bless their fellow-men. Where in all the literature of the world can· we find any teaching more catholic, more humane, than is contained in the parable of the Good Samaritan, wherein Jesus, in opposition to prejudice of race and creed, boldly commends the heterodox outcast because of his humanity to one who probably regarded him as an alien? It is true that Cicero tells us, "Men are Godlike in nothing so much as in doing good to their fellow-creatures." True, also, is it that Mohammed says, "Every good act is charity: your smiling in your brother's face; your putting a wanderer in the right road; your giving water to the thirsty." True he also tells us, "A man's true wealth hereafter is the good he has done in this world to his fellow-men." True the very savage commends kind deeds done among brethren of the same tribe. But in ancient times men were almost always exclusive; and, while they taught love to their neighbours, they also encouraged hatred to their enemies. Nor was the word "neighbour" interpreted with any great liberality; while the word "enemy" included all those beyond one's own land or faith.

The Prophet of Nazareth, on the other hand, looked beyond the children of His own race; and above all else, and, in spite of everything, required kindliness between man and man. He taught, indeed, that those who entertained ill-will, and gave vent to angry feelings against their fellow-men, would be *liable* to the very worst evil that could overtake them. For He saw that those who do one wrong often do further wrong; and that, as one evil leads to another, those who begin by being angry with their brethren are *liable* to go on and on, till at length they may even suffer the extremest punishment of death. So important did Jesus see it was that men should beware lest they took even the first step towards destruction, so necessary did He feel it was that they should guard against anger, so essential did He deem reconciliation between man and man, that He said, in language bolder than that ever used by prophet before His day, "If, therefore, thou art offering thy gift at the *altar*, and there rememberest that thy *brother* hath ought against thee, leave there thy gift before the altar, and go thy way; first be reconciled to thy brother; and then come, and offer thy gift."

And not only do we here see that Jesus desired to show that the beginning of evil should be carefully guarded against, that just as one seed may become a forest, so may anger lead to death; not only do we see that He desired to emphasize the fact, that thought and feeling precede our deeds, that just as the inside of the cup or platter should be cleansed first, so we should before all else cherish kindly thoughts and feelings to those about us; but we also see He wanted to show that we cannot serve God at all while we are doing our neighbours any wrong, nay, while we are *thinking* or *feeling* any wrong concerning our fellow-men.

In the first century, however, as in the nineteenth century, many professors of religion were very far astray from this great truth. Then, as now, men had departed step by step from the path of justice, until they committed such flagrant crimes as devouring widows' houses, which wickedness they thought to condone by saying long prayers. Now, as then, some men seem to believe that right opinion is of the two more important than righteousness of life; and among professed Christians, as among professed Jews, the mere performance of a so-called "religious" duty, though of a purely external character, is often regarded as more needful than kindly deeds done to one another. As in earlier days many paid tithe of mint and anise and cummin, but omitted the weightier matters of the law—justice, mercy, and fidelity,—so, in these later days, many will "perform" most scrupulously what they call "the service of God," while, as if by a law of compensation, they often neglect the barest duties towards the children of the great Father of us all. "Whosoever shall *say*, that property, which according to the law of Moses ought to go to the support of an aged father or mother, is dedicated to God, need not any more help his father or mother, but is free from all further obligation;" so ran the current theology in the days of Jesus. But the Prophet of Nazareth, with largest human heart and noblest sympathy, met this sophistry with stern rebuke, and pressed the claims of man on man with all the energy of His character, bidding His disciples do most for those who needed most. And, judged by the teaching of their Master, men to-day must be pronounced un-

Christian in the same proportion as they neglect these human duties, even though it be to find more time to attend the services of their Church.

In one sense it is probable that Jesus did not intend to be an innovator, and in His day there was less need for nonconformity than now. There was no Act of Uniformity until the religion taught by Jesus had been corrupted, and His method reversed. But now oneness of form has been substituted by the Churches for oneness of spirit. The Prophet of Nazareth, however, was free to stand up in the synagogue, and to speak forth during the hour of worship the word that was burning in His inmost heart, though, were He here to-day, this freedom would be denied Him by our Established Church. All history teaches that, while the priestly influence tends to dwarf our manhood, the prophetic influence tends to develop what is best in man; and, therefore, this latest and greatest Prophet of Israel called men from the letter to the spirit, from outward appearance to inner realities, from form to life. Ever was His voice raised in favour of kindly feeling between man and man, and, to this day, there is no religion of humanity like the pure religion of Christ. True Christianity is Divine, because it is so intensely human. Not only were the sympathies of Jesus ever on the side of the weak, the downtrodden, the oppressed; but they were warm towards everything that was noblest and best in man. So far did He push this human tendency in religion that He carried it into the very Temple service; and, when two duties appeared to present themselves simultaneously—the one due to God, the other to man,—He did not hesitate to apply that human principle which underlies His every word and deed. Here, as everywhere, He remained true to His own teaching, and declared that what was deemed the service of God must be kept for a time in abeyance, that the service of the weak, who stood in need of our aid, may not even be delayed. "First be reconciled to thy brother, and then come and offer thy gift." Jesus knew that God can bide His time while we serve our neighbours; and we ought to know that no duty can ever be more pressing than true charity or love to man, and that if we allow any kindly service to a fellow-creature to wait at the door of our devotions, we are neither true to God, nor true to man; neither are we true followers of Christ.

We are told that "the scribes required restitution in money matters, but that, in other things, they held that gifts and sacrifices would expiate all offences not cognisable by the judge." But we read of Jesus that the multitudes were astonished at His teaching; for He taught them as one having authority, and *not* as their scribes. And, surely, this is true when He puts reconciliation between man and man, in point of time at least, before sacrifice, and what is often regarded as "the *service* of God." Can we say, indeed, that eighteen centuries of progress have carried us beyond this teaching of the lowly Galilean? We have organised Churches; we have built schools and colleges; we have founded

Bible and temperance societies; we have sent missionaries to all parts of the world; and we have often considered ourselves the most Christian of nations. But one thing we have not done,—we have not yet fully learned the great lesson taught throughout the words of Jesus; not yet have we learned to live like brothers, and to love our fellow-men. The so-called Christian Church has split up into a hundred fragments, each clinging to its own peculiarities, as though they constituted "the Gospel of God," and were alone needful for the well-being of man; and yet, where our own flesh and blood has suffered most, whether in the olden days of bond-service, or in these modern days of fierce competition, when many free men are without decent homes and the plainest necessary food,—those who profess and call themselves Christians too often, like the priest and Levite, pass by on the other side. Have we not been told by a Member of Parliament, at a conference on the London poor, held at the Mansion House, that it is "impossible to abolish poverty and stamp out rookeries, unless you abolish *original sin*, and you could never do that"? But Jesus, in dealing with the poor, never said anything about original sin, and we know that such a thing does not exist. True, we read in the Fourth Gospel that the Pharisees said, "This multitude, which knoweth not the law, are accursed;" but Jesus said, "Come unto Me, all ye that labour and are heavy laden." Indeed, He tells us, "That servant, which knew his lord's will, and made not ready, nor did according to his will, shall be beaten with many stripes; but he that knew not, and did things worthy of stripes, shall be beaten with few stripes;" and, therefore, we conclude that those who have inherited the greatest number of evil tendencies, when they do a given wrong, commit *less sin*, and not more than those who have been more fortunate in their ancestors. The great Teacher said unto His disciples, "Verily I say unto you, it is hard for a rich man to enter into the kingdom of heaven;" and that saying remains true, even unto this day. It is easy for us to fancy that the evils which surround us cannot be helped; it is easy for us to think that they are due to something which cannot be remedied; it is, therefore, easy for us to leave our less fortunate neighbours to their fate, while we eat and drink and make merry. Jesus, however, loved and served the poor and outcast; but now many who call themselves His followers get rich at their expense, because they only love and help themselves. Jesus knew nothing about our theology with its original sin! But we go to church, as the scribes and Pharisees did before us, to pray for our own souls, and leave the poor to wallow in what we are pleased to call "original sin," as a preparation for damnation hereafter! Then, surely, that religion which seeks before all else for right feeling and conduct between man and man is the religion which we still stand in need of—a religion which, if really accepted, would soon sweep away one half of the evils which flesh is heir to, and help men to bear the other half that remained.

And this religion we might accept to-day if we were content with the actual teaching of Jesus—a religion intensely human in its tendency, and beyond all other forms of faith calculated to make us better and kinder to one another; a religion, too, which is eminently practical and calculated to bring us face to face with present duties; a religion which would elevate and bless all mankind, and knit together every race and people in a universal brotherhood, wherein poverty and vice would be unknown.

> "O brother man, fold to thy heart thy brother!
>   Where pity dwells, the peace of God is there;
> To worship rightly is to love each other,
>   Each smile a hymn, each kindly deed a prayer.
> Follow with reverent steps the great example
>   Of Him Whose holy work was doing good;
> So shall the wide earth seem our Father's temple,
>   Each loving life a psalm of gratitude.
> Then shall all shackles fall; the stormy clangour
>   Of wild war music o'er the earth shall cease;
> Love shall tread out the baleful fire of anger,
>   And in its ashes plant the tree of peace."

CHAPTER X.

THE FOLLOWERS OF JESUS.

ALL Christians declare that they believe in Jesus; all Christians profess that they are His disciples; and yet the Church is still to-day split up into many and conflicting parties, instead of presenting one united front in the presence of the ignorance and evil and sin by which we are surrounded. But although the various sects of Christendom are so numerous, they may, I think, be roughly classified according to five different schools.

And, in the first place, we find those who, either in theory or practice, follow what they call "the Church" as the supreme authority in matters pertaining to religion. This party constantly speak of "the Church" as "The Church of Christ;" and assume that it was founded by the great Prophet of Nazareth, and, therefore, possesses the power to settle by its decrees all points not only of ritual, but even of doctrine. Is there, however, any good evidence for this assumption? Is there any evidence that "the Church" existed in the days of Jesus? Do we know that Jesus ever desired, or intended, to found any such institution? Must we not conclude, from all that we read in our Gospels, that

Jesus was not only born and educated as a Jew, but that He also lived and died in the faith of His fathers? According to the Second Gospel, when one of the scribes came and asked Him, "What commandment is the first of all?" Jesus answered, "The first is, Hear, *O Israel;* the Lord *our God*, the Lord is One," which seems a clear indication that He looked upon Himself as within the fold of Israel, and as accepting the monotheistic faith of His people. That this great Prophet sought to reform Judaism is perfectly clear; but is there any reason for our supposing that He ever left the communion of Israel, and then sought to found what many now call "the Church"? It is true that the word "Church" occurs about one hundred times in the New Testament; but is it not probable that the only two passages (both of which are in our First Gospel), in which Jesus is made to refer to "the Church," are of later date than His lifetime? Nay, is it not morally certain that this is the case with the latter of these two passages (Matt. xviii.), wherein, as Alford says, the "ecclesia" is "certainly not the Jewish synagogue"? For, is there the slightest evidence to suppose that, at this early time, there was any congregation of Christians in existence which met together apart from the Jews? Can we, moreover, suppose that Jesus, Whose ministry was chiefly spent among the "lost sheep of the house of Israel," and Who chose a publican as one of His first disciples, used the words, "Let him be unto thee as the Gentile and the publican"? Yet Catholics, whether Romanists or Anglicans, although they profess and call themselves Christians, do not make their ultimate appeal to the teaching of Jesus, but to "the Church" of which He knew nothing, and could know nothing, seeing that it had not begun to exist till after He passed away. Then, again, this school or party in the Christian Church does not adopt the method of Jesus. The great Nazarene cared but little for tradition, or for forms and ceremonies; but with the followers of "the Church" traditions and ceremonies are often considered very important, while the principles and the doctrines of Jesus are more or less frequently ignored.

But, according to Matthew Arnold, the mass of the English nation take, not "the Church," but "the Bible" as their supreme rule of faith. These people frequently scorn tradition, and will only build their religion on what they deem the pure word of God! Is this, however, a safe and tenable position? The Bible, no doubt, is the most remarkable collection of books the world has ever seen. It is supposed to give us the history of Creation from the cradle of the human race, to take us into the very workshop of the Almighty, when the earth was without form and void, and darkness was upon the face of the deep. It represents the universe in the first stage of its existence, as clay in the hands of the Potter to be fashioned according to His mind and will. We read in its pages that light came out of darkness at the word of Jehovah. This volume, too, professes to solve the riddle of our existence, to account for the origin of good and evil. It represents God, in the infancy of the world, as walking this earth, and holding direct converse with the children of men. And, now to-day, the teaching of these old and venerated books has pervaded the literature of at least two continents. The historian, the novelist, the newspaper writer, the man of science,—all draw inspiration from this storehouse of wisdom. Is it any wonder, then, that the great bulk of our people appeal to the Bible as their great authority in matters pertaining to religion? But the Bible is not simply a book; it is not even a mere collection of books. It is a whole literature in itself, and contains all that was deemed most worthy among the writings of the Hebrews, and for this reason, if for no other, has lived on through the ages. But in Israel it was looked upon, not as private, but as public property, and was kept in the hands of public custodians, who from time to time edited and re-edited its various parts. We shall be wrong, indeed, if we imagine that even a single book, like Genesis or the Psalms, was all written by one person. Some books, too, both in the Old Testament and in the New Testament times, have been lost wholly or in part, though in some cases parts of the older books have been preserved and incorporated in later ones. But, as Matthew Arnold tells us: "There was a time when books were read as part of the Bible which are in no Bible now; there was a time when books which are in every Bible now were by many disallowed as genuine parts of the Bible. St. Athanasius rejected the Book of Esther, and the Greek Christianity of the East repelled the Apocalypse, and the Latin Christianity of the West repelled the Epistle to the Hebrews." Did not Luther, too, say that the Epistle of James was an epistle of straw? And now we all know that the Bible is a complete literature, composed of works of various dates and merits, ought we any longer to appeal to its authority, as though we thought it all equally trustworthy in every part as a guide to life and conduct? For this rough and ready method, which takes the Bible—the whole Bible, and nothing but the Bible—as the supreme authority in religion, has led, and still leads, many people far away from the truth. No man does, no man can, at one and the same time, follow the whole teaching of a volume which sets forth the thoughts and the feelings of so many various ages and different degrees of civilisation. And not only so; but, having so large a storehouse to select from, many pick out the least worthy parts, while they pass by its higher and holier teaching. How many an unholy war has been carried on under the cloak of the authority of some parts of the Old Testament Scriptures! And, probably, as long as men worship the Bible, so long will they delight in war, and find excuses for it. Are not soldiers to-day often the most "orthodox" of Christians? Are they not frequently the most regular in their attendance at church? Nay, has not the Bible been appealed to by the advocates of slavery? Do not the Latter Day Saints of Salt Lake City still appeal to its authority as sanctioning their own peculiar customs? But the time has now come for plain speaking on this subject. For we all know, and knowing, should, therefore, admit, that while the teaching of the Bible on the whole is grand and beautiful, yet its morality is sometimes by no means of a very high tone. It, therefore, becomes not the disciples of Jesus to appeal to its pages indiscriminately, as though its every teaching was the word of God.

There is another class of Christians who, though they may not dwell so much on the Old Testament as on the New Testament, perhaps follow the apostles more than they follow Jesus. These we may distinguish as "Theological Christians," though often misnamed "Evangelical." This school or party is found both among Churchmen and Dissenters, although it took its rise in our Establishment, and is due in all probability to the thirty-nine Articles of Religion contained in the Book of Common Prayer. For who that is at all familiar with the Gospels can read these Articles without perceiving that they are deduced almost entirely from the epistles, and that the teaching of Jesus is conspicuous by its absence from them? I am not saying whether the Articles in themselves are either true or false; but I do affirm that they give us no approximate notion of the message proclaimed by the Galilean Prophet. So also we find that the teaching of Jesus is almost entirely absent from the Creeds of our Established Church; and, moreover, we even find in the Creeds themselves a development of doctrine each step in which departs further and further from the simplicity of the Gospel.

We now come to a large class of Christians who, in

seeking to follow Jesus, seem to miss the very pith and marrow of His teaching, and thus practically reject His message. In the First Epistle to the Corinthians Paul says, "We preach Christ;" and, again, in the Second Epistle to the Corinthians he says, "We preach not ourselves, but Christ Jesus." Now, all will agree that the last thing that a preacher should do is to preach himself. So far, then, Paul was undoubtedly right, inasmuch as he did not preach himself. But by whose authority did he preach Christ? Are men who preach Christ instead of preaching God really following Jesus? The Prophet of Nazareth, so far as we know, never commissioned His disciples to preach Christ. Jesus, like Paul, preached not Himself; but, unlike Paul, He preached not Christ but the Father. In the First Gospel we read that, when Jesus began to preach, His message was, "Repent ye, for the kingdom of heaven is at hand;" or, as we read in the Second Gospel, "The time is fulfilled, and the kingdom of God is at hand: repent ye, and believe the good news." So, likewise, when He sent forth His twelve disciples He said to them, "As ye go, preach, saying, The kingdom of heaven is at hand." Who, then, gave "the Church" authority to follow Paul rather than Jesus, and to put Christ in the place of God? Surely, following Jesus is doing as Jesus did; and He preached not Christ but God. The teaching of Jesus is full of this message concerning God, Whom He calls "Our Father." God, according to this great Prophet, is the Father, and man the son; and, therefore,

He teaches that He too, "the Son of Man," like each disciple, is a Son of God. Must it not follow, then, that all those (however good may be their intentions) who seek to glorify Christ by putting Him in the place of God, in so doing practically reject the message of the Prophet of Nazareth?

But is there not an ever-increasing number of thoughtful men and women in all the Churches who are coming to see this great fact more and more clearly every day? Are there not now many people, both among those who are called "heterodox," and among those called "orthodox," who are seeking to follow Jesus by doing what Jesus did—people who, like Him, regard God as "Our Father," and who, like Him, worship the Father alone? "The hour cometh, and *now* is, when the true worshippers shall worship the Father in spirit and truth, for such doth the Father seek to be His worshippers. God is a Spirit; and they that worship Him must worship Him in spirit and in truth." And are not they "the true worshippers" who, like Jesus, worship the Father alone; and are they not also, like Jesus, sons of God? Are not they "the true worshippers" who pray to the Father, as Jesus prayed to the Father; and who, like Jesus, approach God without any mediator, but simply as children? The great Prophet from Galilee admitted neither Book nor Church to be master of His heart and conscience; but, while treasuring all the wise and good sayings of those who had lived before His time, trusted for guidance to the ever-present inspiration of the Spirit of God. And why should not those who seek to be His disciples do the same? All Christians agree that men must have faith in Jesus. But, if this faith is to be deep and true, if it is to be perfect, ought it not to include faith in His method, faith in His principles, faith in His doctrines; and ought it not likewise to embrace faith in His character—a character which grows out of His method, His principles, His doctrines; a character which is nourished by a child-like dependence on "Our Father," and a genuine desire to do His will? In the First and Second Gospel we read that Jesus stretched forth His hand towards His disciples, and said, "Behold, My mother and My brethren! For whosoever shall do the will of My Father which is in heaven, he is My brother, and sister, and mother." Then the true followers of Jesus are not the men who merely accept, or reject, this or that dogma of the Churches, but those who find their meat and drink in doing the will of God; and, according to this great Prophet, it is the will of God that we regard Him as "Our Father," and His children as our brethren—brethren of Jesus.

Not that it is necessary for the disciple to see eye to eye with Jesus in mere matters of opinion, any more than He saw eye to eye with all the wise and good men who lived before His day. Neither is it essential for men now who are brethren to think all alike. No mere matter of opinion can ever be of the essence of religion; for, as we all know, some opinions which the Churches once held, they have now quite outgrown, while other opinions, still deemed important by some, an ever-increasing number of good men and women are ceasing to hold. Is it not, indeed, ever true in all matters pertaining to religion, that those things of which we may be most certain are precisely those which are the most important? And, is it not what we *know*—know by our own personal experience—which really makes for life? If, then, as Herbert Spencer says, "Of the three phases through which human opinion passes—the unanimity of the ignorant, the disagreement of the inquiring, and the unanimity of the wise—it is manifest that the second is the parent of the third," why should not Christians seek for unity, not by requiring men to accept dogmas, about which so many good men have grave doubts, but by building alone on those simple and grand truths concerning which most good people are more or less fully agreed? Why should they not, leaving aside all creeds and articles of religion, insist alone on the commandments of Jesus as the bond of Christian fellowship, being content that all should agree in seeking to love God and serve their fellow-men?

> "Help us to help each other, Lord,
>   Each other's cross to bear;
> Let each his friendly aid afford,
>   And feel his brother's care.
> Help us to build each other up,
>   Our little stock improve;
> Increase our faith, confirm our hope,
>   And perfect us in love!"

PRINTED BY
HAZELL WATSON, AND VINEY, LD.,
LONDON AND AYLESBURY.

www.ingramcontent.com/pod-product-compliance
Lightning Source LLC
Chambersburg PA
CBHW021944160426
43195CB00011B/1218